'Can You Pass The Acid Test?' – 1966 signed poster from the collection of Mike Zaidlin – sixties.com ➲

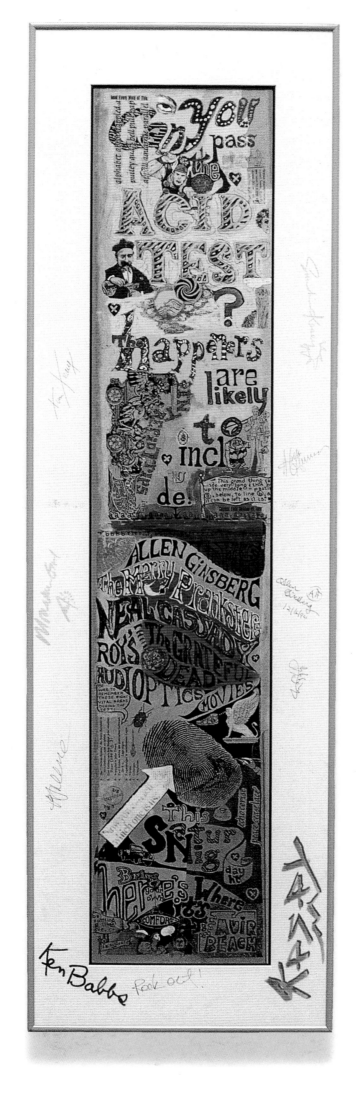

HIGH ART

TED OWEN
DENISE DICKSON

A HISTORY OF THE
PSYCHEDELIC
——— POSTER ———

ACKNOWLEDGMENTS

Grateful thanks are made to the following for making this book possible:
Alan and Debbie Caplan for their patience and understanding, Gary and
Laura Grimshaw, Stanley "Mouse" Miller, Randy Tuten, John Platt,
Walter Medeiros, Chet Helms, Bill Graham Presents, Jerry Pompili and
Rebecca Nichols at BGP, Michael English, Alan Forbes, Mark Arminski,
Mark McCloud, Gene Anthony, Roger Dixon, the San Francisco Museum
Of Modern Art, and a big thank you to all of the poster artists for being there.

What a long strange trip it's been.

Love, Peace and Power – museums beware!

Published by: Sanctuary Publishing Limited,
The Colonnades, 82 Bishops Bridge Road, London W2 6BB

Designed by: Storm Thorgerson, Jon Crossland and John McGill

Printed in Hong Kong

Copyright: Ted Owen, 1999

Text by Walter Medeiros, © 1976, 1998 the San Francisco Museum Of Modern
Art, originally appeared in the exhibition catalogue San Francisco Rock Poster Art,
published by the museum in 1976.
Essay by John Platt, p125-130, © John Platt.

Posters: all images used in this work are subject to copyright clearance with the artists or
copyright holders. The Bill Graham posters BG 6, BG 7, BG 9, BG 10, BG 17, BG 18, BG 34
and BG 41 are all © Bill Graham Presents 1966; BG 45, BG 48, BG 50, BG 51, BG 53, BG 54,
BG 56, BG 57, BG 59, BG 65, BG 76, BG 89 and BG 90 all © BGP 1967; BG 105, BG 109, BG
121, BG 127, BG 128, BG 131, BG 136, BG 140, BG 146 and BG 152 all © BGP 1968; BG
154, BG 168, BG 174, BG 180, BG 181, BG 185, BG 199 and BG 206 all © BGP 1969; BG 225
and BG 250 © BGP 1970; BG 279, BG 280 and BG 287 all © BGP 1971; Avalon Ballroom
posters © Family Dog Productions, dba of Chester Helms, 771 Bush Street, San Francisco,
CA 94108 USA; all Neon Rose posters © Victor Moscoso; all Hapshash posters © Nigel Way-
mouth and Michael English; all Gary Grimshaw posters © Gary Grimshaw at earthlink.net.

CONTENTS

ONE : INTRODUCTION : 9
EARLY ARTISTIC INFLUENCES : 20

TWO : THE AMERICAN SCENE : 31
PROMOTERS AND VENUES : 38
POSTER ARTISTS : 52

THREE : THE BRITISH SCENE : 111
POSTER ARTISTS : 133

FOUR : THE NEW WAVE : 149

FIVE : COLLECTING PSYCHEDELIC POSTERS : 163

PREFACE   Over my past thirty years of work as an artist I have encountered very few people who

have been completely honest with me at all times, and Ted Owen is one of them.

His assessments of value have always been accurate and whatever he has promised to deliver has arrived on time and intact,

and believe me, in this business that has been most unusual.

Ted truly loves and is deeply committed to promoting psychedelic and rock 'n' roll posters. He made a conscious effort

to meet and spend a substantial amount of time with me and a number of the other poster artists – including Stanley Mouse,

Gary Grimshaw and Alan Forbes – to learn more about this artform and our experiences in producing it. Ted also has featured

our work in many of the Bonhams rock 'n' roll memorabilia auctions. His efforts to enhance the standing of psychedelic and

rock 'n' roll poster art in the public consciousness have born fruit, including the organisation and promotion of two recent,

highly successful Bonhams auctions which involved only the sale of posters.

I have no doubt that this book will also further the public understanding and appreciation for psychedelic and

rock 'n' roll poster art, by showing and discussing many of these works of great beauty which have been created over the

past thirty years. What is equally important, however, is that the reader will discover that the growth of the form is ongo-

ing and expanding, with many poster artists (both the "old guard" and younger contributors) continuing to create excit-

ing, vibrant and fun posters for the enjoyment of all.

Randy Tuten, American poster artist

Tim Leary, Millbrook Mansion – 1967
PHOTO: GENE ANTHONY

TURN ON, TUNE IN, DROP OUT!

The early Sixties saw two or three years of spectacular economic growth in the West. The increase in world trade at the beginning of the decade was unprecedented in modern times, more than matching the increase which marked the great days of Empire in the first dozen years of the twentieth century. Inevitably, the mood of the period reflected the changed circumstance of economic expansion. A new liberalism spread across Europe and America as more money, more time and a greater variety of goods and services became available to people. The relatively narrow horizons encouraged by austerity and Cold War paranoia in the Fifties broadened under the influence of cheap travel, new and powerful communications technologies and the pressure of industries seeking new markets.

In Britain, the satire boom, the Profumo affair, the popularity of The Beatles and a revolution in fashion, spreading from small boutiques in Carnaby Street and the King's Road, all heralded profound changes in mass society. Old attitudes and stale traditions were being swept aside as rampant consumerism encouraged a sense of experimentation and freedom in sexual morality, clothes, hairstyles, music, art and politics.

In the United States – where conditions were significantly different – the changing mood of the early Sixties was evidenced by the growth of folk-protest music, the increasing acceptance of "beatnik" ideals, the burgeoning appeal of modern or "cool" jazz and the birth of the radical student movement. Towering above all these, perhaps, was the fact of John F Kennedy's election to the presidency in 1960.

IN THE PRESIDENT'S STEPS   **Kennedy was young, good-looking, apparently liberal and – a first for the US presidency** – a Catholic. As many commentators have noted, Kennedy's assassination in 1963 provides at least a partial explanation of The Beatles' subsequent success with younger generations in America. They stepped into the vacuum Kennedy left and came to symbolise everything that the president had once symbolised: youthfulness, success, good humour, good looks, playful boyishness, innocence combined with native cunning, hope for the future and a crucial unconventionality.

With Kennedy and The Beatles, the line between politics and showbiz became all but invisible. Both seemed to represent a new and popular urge to democracy and the overthrow of restrictive national boundaries. And rock – accepted as the form of showbiz for the young – was the perfect vehicle for the aspirations of those who were beginning to see themselves as the first settlers in a Brave New World. The possibilities were seemingly endless.

Indeed, rock music's role in the changing mood of the Sixties can hardly be overestimated. The new electronic technologies that shaped rock and grew up on its back helped create new patterns of consumption and new styles of music. Fifties rock 'n' roll was relatively unsophisticated in its aspirations, but, by the time Phil Spector was producing his "little symphonies for kids" with The Ronettes and The Crystals, rock had developed a sense of its own artistic potential. Developments in broadcasting, recording and amplification technology would help fulfil this potential, while the widespread availability of cheap hi-fi (also made possible by rock's enormous popularity) gave rock artistic credibility by enabling the private consumption of crafted work.

Perhaps even more significant was the way that rock tied in with radical politics, becoming an instrument for stirring the consciences of the young. Consumerism created its own contradictions. In making ideas and technologies widely available for the sake of profit alone, it was unable to discourage more radical ideas and the use of technologies in a struggle against the profit system.

The key figure in this process in the early Sixties was undeniably Bob Dylan, who had renounced rock 'n' roll at the end of the previous decade to pursue a more "committed" kind of music. Dylan's involvement in the early Sixties' movement for black Civil Rights made him a political figure. But that movement – like the anti-Vietnam War movement that followed it – was essentially a part of the same general process of liberalisation that lay behind Sixties consumerism.

WORLD OF HOPE? One of the crucial aspects of this liberalisation was that it confirmed the end of imperialism. From the beginning of the Sixties, Third World cultures were no longer reviled as alien, inferior and merely exploitable. On the contrary, they were promoted (at least, in public) as exotic, interesting, future partners in the worldwide adventure of industrialisation. On a more superficial level, the East was famed as the source of spicy foods, colourful clothes, profound ideas and fascinating art – all of which, in one form or another, could be gainfully exchanged for dollars and pounds.

Although overt imperialism was at an end, this did not deter Western nations continuing to exploit and oppress former colonies and colonised peoples. The American blacks were such a people, and the Civil Rights movement was seen as an essentially anti-imperialist struggle. Blacks became "Afro-Americans", some converted to Islam and many argued for a

Trips Festival,
Longshoreman's Hall
– January 1966
PHOTO: GENE ANTHONY

future independent of – even separate from – white America. The Vietnam War, too, was seen as an anti-imperialist struggle; as the Sixties progressed, supporters of the struggles of such colonial peoples – whose ideas had been allowed free range in the liberal atmosphere of an expansionary West – began to see that very expansionary West as an ogre.

Dylan and many of his contemporaries turned that message into song. They promoted their vision of a better world in terms that pitted the values of industrial, urbanised societies against the "more human" values of (a probably imaginary) Third World and rural peasantry. Folk music, country blues, marijuana, Tibetan bells, Indian incense, Islam and Buddhism all became fashionable, as did many other products of Third World and rural societies. These were the overt symbols of opposition to the oppressive technocracy of the West.

Dylan – who turned The Beatles on to marijuana in 1964 and thereby opened at least one set of floodgates – was canny enough to understand technology's contradictory nature. His going electric in 1965 seemed a sell-out to many radicals and folk musicians, but it was, for Dylan, a route to vaster audiences than any traditional folk musicians could previously have dreamed of.

Into this ferment of new music, political radicalism, colourful clothes and unconventional lifestyles stepped LSD – the most powerful hallucinogenic drug known. Through the patronage of people like the novelist Aldous Huxley and the philosopher of religion Alan Watts – as well as a number of experimentally inclined psychiatrists and psychologists – LSD had already gained something of a reputation as a wonder drug. Huxley and Watts promoted a quasi-religious view of LSD, linking it to mysticism and the ancient ritual use of other hallucinogens such as the psilocybin ("magic") mushroom, mescaline and hashish. Others had investigated the drug's use in more mundane problem-solving or therapeutic contexts. Those who had come across LSD by the onset of the Sixties were convinced of its potential for changing human awareness on an individual level.

The single most important thing about LSD, however, was that it was a synthetic substance – a technological product which seemed to have profoundly humanising effects. Here was the acute contradiction of Sixties economic expansion embodied and resolved in an odourless, colourless, tasteless liquid: LSD was a mass-produced commodity in the exclusive service of the spiritual and creative lives of human beings.

The drug's messiah, psychologist Timothy Leary, was sacked from Harvard University in 1962 for spreading the LSD gospel. Travelling through California, Mexico and New York, he propounded his philosophy of "the psychedelic revolution" (the term psychedelic – literally, "mind manifesting" – was coined by an early LSD-experimenter to describe the drug's effects). Leary left a trail of converts whose attitudes to LSD's "consciousness-expanding" possibilities varied from the playful to the deadly earnest. Almost everybody who came in touch with LSD in those days did take one of Leary's messages at face value: "turn on, tune in and drop out" became the slogan of the age.

A common effect of the drug was to heighten the senses and break down the barriers to perception. Colours would glow, sounds would linger and resonate; sometimes one stimulus would

provoke quite an unexpected response so that music would become translated into imagined visions. Rock music – loud, simple, often repetitive and highly rhythmic – became the favoured soundtrack for the LSD "trip". New performers emerged in the "Acid Tests", "Trips Festivals", "Be-Ins" and "Freak-Outs" that started in the mid Sixties as anarchic events to occupy the sensation-hungry tripper through an eight- to twelve-hour experience. These performers – notably The Grateful Dead in America and Pink Floyd in Britain – cultivated a style which depended on simple chord structures, massive amplification and much repetitive improvisation. Their performances were often accompanied by light shows using slides, spotlights and bits of film, and audiences were encouraged to dance, wear make-up and flowing clothes and generally pursue as many different stimuli as possible.

By 1967, LSD itself had been made almost universally illegal. Yet the psychedelic lifestyle was in full swing, a rendered-down liquor strained off from the casserole of economic expansion, the resurgence of rock and LSD itself. Indeed, psychedelia was most significant as a popular fashion towards the end of the Sixties, when beads, bells, paisley shirts, cut-rate Eastern religions and flower-power pop finally found their niche in the expanded marketplace.

In 1955, as these societal winds of change began to increase in force, British psychiatrist Dr Humphrey Osmond was deeply engaged in the study of substances which altered human consciousness, including among many others, cannabis, mescaline and Lysergic Acid Diethylamide (known as LSD 25). To describe the experience resulting from the ingestion of these substances he developed the word "psychedelic" by combining the Greek

THE IMPACT OF LSD words "psyche", meaning "mind, spirit or soul", and "delos" meaning "clearly apparent or seen". He believed that joining the two words in this manner would best describe the experience of heightened awareness that use of psychedelics evoked.

Osmond's conclusions coincided with results reached by Aldous Huxley, who had also been researching the effects of mescaline for his book *The Doors Of Perception*. Huxley asserted that the most basic aspects of the psychedelic experience were the open eye, the naked touch, the intensification and vivification of sound, smell and taste. The ability to turn on the senses, to escape the everyday conditioning had traditionally been the exclusive mountain domain of the high priest, sage, holy man, or shaman, attainable only after years of study and sacrifice. Beginning in the 1960s we now had a whole generation of young people able to turn on this psychedelic experience by the single act of ingesting a single sugar cube, tiny piece of blotter paper or acetate saturated with LSD.

➲ 'Felix' acid blotter art
➲ Ken Kesey – 1966 PHOTO: GENE ANTHONY
➲ 'Mad Hatter' acid blotter art

LSD had been leaking out from experimental laboratories and into society far too long to remain a well-kept secret. Thanks in large part to the efforts of Michael Hollingsworth, Timothy Leary, Ken Kesey[1] and a host of others, people from all walks of life were given the opportunity to participate in the psychedelic experience. (A small measure of thanks should also go to the United States government which provided the funds for the LSD experiments which introduced Ken Kesey to LSD, after which Kesey and the Merry Pranksters turned on countless others.) Artists, musicians, film makers, politicians, students, a wide spectrum of curious people of all backgrounds and experiences were anxious to try the new wonder substance which promised immediate enlightenment, or as some trumpeted, "instant Nirvana".

The Beatles were also an early and major force, hinting on the *Revolver* LP that they were at the very centre of the psychedelic revolution. "Turn off your mind, relax and float down stream, it is not dying," says John Lennon, experiencing the death/rebirth trip familiar to many who have taken the LSD experience seriously. The release of *Sgt Pepper's Lonely Hearts Club Band* saw The Beatles fully emerging from the psychedelic closet. It was a colourful celebration: "We'd love to turn you on," they sang to a world absorbed in war, repression and persecution.

LSD gave freedom to the Sixties youth culture. The kids were disillusioned with the war in Vietnam, racism, class distinctions and parental and governmental controls. Their rebellion and rage were vented through music, dance and poetry as well as protest, as the soul and spirit of a generation could be heard throughout the world with the psychedelic poster as its symbol.

Some thirty years later, there remains an underground, highly secret, but very active LSD movement, and there are many people of all ages who still use LSD, although it is considered to be an illegal drug. Of equal significance is the fact that the medium upon which it is delivered, blotter paper, has itself become an ever-expanding artform. This phenomenon had remained almost wholly anecdotal until Mark McCloud of San Francisco began to show his collection of hundreds of pieces of blotter acid art to the world.

1: Ken Kesey: *author of* One Flew Over The Cuckoo's Nest *and* Once A Great Notion

Until the late 1960s and early Seventies, acid had been placed onto sugar cubes, packed into capsules, or pressed into tablets. At that time clandestine manufacturers learned that if they dipped blotter paper into a solution of LSD, they could perfectly control the strength and consistency of each individual dose. Over time an "industry" standard in size and potency developed so that most full sheets of acid are eleven inches long by eight and a half inches wide, and perforated into 1,000 quarter inch squares. The amount of LSD in each square is minute, only one millionth of a gram.

The other advantage to blotter paper as a medium for delivering acid is that it presented a perfect surface upon which any image could be printed. Images were selected by the LSD manufacturers to provide a unique, but anonymous, stamp of authenticity, or as a statement or prophecy as to the nature of the trip which the consumer of that brand would experience. A specific image also served as a statement of quality control, a "guarantee" that a square of this product was of the same dosage strength and quality as any other carrying this same insignia.

The images utilised varied from the sacred (Jesus on the cross) to the spiritual (Ganesha, the elephant-headed God of the Hindus), to the profane (Felix the Cat). Also depicted were musical figures, such as Ozzy Osbourne, and reproductions of images related to The Grateful Dead, political figures including Mikhail Gorbachev, and cartoon figures of the times ranging from Batman to Beavis and Butthead. Sometimes the image was a warning (or boast) about the strength and quality of the acid, such as a skull and crossbones.

In many instances, the blotter acid artists used an extremely reduced stat image to provide the same unique and complete image on each of the quarter inch squares on the sheet, for example 1,000 identical yin/yang symbols. Other times the whole sheet contains a single image, such as Alice stepping through the looking glass into Wonderland, so that each individual square is like a small piece in a jigsaw puzzle.

Thus McCloud's collection features mandala-like figures in myriad colours, shapes as variant as flying saucers, Mickey Mouse in a sorcerer's hat (from the cartoon classic *Fantasia*), and political statements as in a sheet on which each square contains a tiny but absolutely perfect reproduction of the official FBI seal. The images also tended to illustrate the split within the secret world of LSD between Timothy Leary's Millbrook group, who viewed LSD as a key to heightened consciousness leading to spiritual enlightenment, and Ken Kesey's Merry Pranksters, who viewed acid as a great cosmic goof, as a means for fun and adventure on an unprecedented level.

Single blotter sheets of various designs are now sold by memorabilia retailers and at auctions. Some, such as those signed by Timothy Leary before his recent death, have brought as much as £1,500. McCloud has exhibited his collection in museums and galleries which have recognised that this is essentially a unique form of folk art. They understand, as do collectors, that the design of blotter acid takes great creativity, including the selection of some specific pre-existing imagery, and the utilisation of innovative graphic techniques to place it on the paper in exactly the correct proportions.

↻ 'Beavis And Butthead' acid blotter art
↺ 'Alice Through The Looking Glass' acid blotter art
↻ 'Tim Leary', signed acid blotter art

EARLY ARTISTIC INFLUENCES

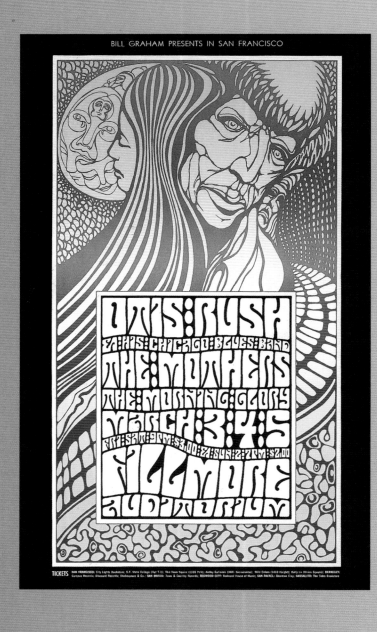

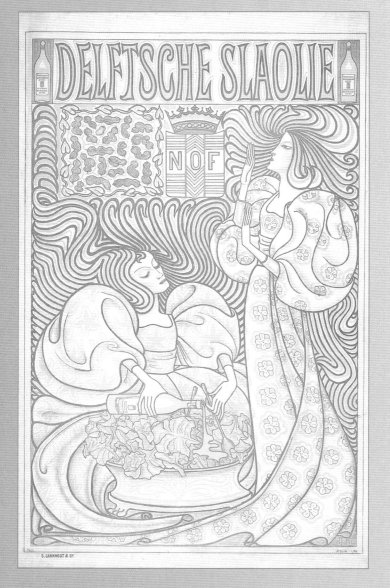

◐◑ Wes Wilson – 1967 BG 53

◑ Jan Toorop – 1895

➲ 'The Sound', Winterland and Fillmore
Auditorium, Wes Wilson – 1966 BG 29

◐◑ 'Nord Express',
AM Cassandre – 1910

◑ 'Normandie',
AM Cassandre – 1935

◑ Randy Tuten – 1969 BG 174

It is no secret that throughout time, artists have scoured books, museums and other historical sources to develop their styles and to find inspiration from the philosophies and works of the past. The psychedelic artists were certainly no different. Stanley Mouse and Alton Kelley passed many days roaming together through art museums and examining books in libraries. The early Virginia City Red Dog Saloon posters were undoubtedly influenced by Victorian play-bills, and the Mouse/Kelley collaboration on the Family Dog poster known as 'Girl With Green Hair' clearly reflects the works of legendary French poster artist Alphonse Mucha (1860-1939). American poster artist Randy Tuten freely admits that he was fascinated, and undoubtedly influenced by the works of Hendrick Cassiers (1858-1944). Cassiers' poster and other art thrust the viewer into the ambience of the sea-going ships of an earlier era, with depictions of certain of the great ocean liners and steam ships of the time, while other works incorporated images of the great Zeppelins (as in the Brussels Exhibition poster of 1910). Those earlier representations of sea and air travel are reflected in a number of Randy Tuten's posters, including that for the 1977 Led Zeppelin concert at the Oakland, California Coliseum, and the poster by John Pasche for The Rolling Stones' 1970 European tour which utilised nautical themes.

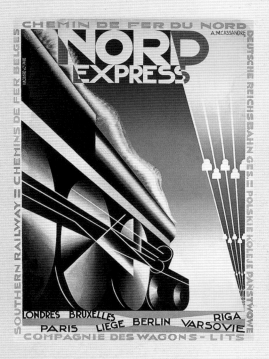

The works of the "Belle Époque" artists from Belgium (1880-1920) formed the primary historical sources for the poster artists who flourished in the last forty years of this century. The efforts of these visionaries of an earlier time generally mirrored their active involvement in, and focus upon "cutting edge" social, economic, political and artistic issues of their era. They provided a new attitude in which, "On all fronts the battle against the ordinary was fought." The beauty in the ideas and techniques of the artists and the highly honed craft of the lithographers of the Belle Époque, as well as their expressions of fresh attitudes toward the issues of their day, were in some measure reflected by all of the young, formidable new psychedelic poster artists.

➲ 'Girl With Green Hair', Alton Kelley and Stanley Mouse, FD 29

↻ 'Book Of Dreams' Alton Kelley and Stanley Mouse – 1976

↻ Poster for the 1910 International Exposition, Brussels, Creten – 1906

↻↻ 'Bugatti' , AM Cassandre – circa 1925

Beginning in the 1960s, the frequent need for dance/event posters which were not tied to ordinary commerce or traditional "straightforward" print advertising created a new universe of possibilities for the psychedelic artists. They were permitted to utilise their unrestricted imaginations, as well as to draw further inspiration from the works of the great artists of previous eras. For example, look closely at the Victor Creten poster designed for the Exhibition Universelle De Bruxelles, 1906-1910, and then compare it to the 1976 Mouse/Kelley artwork for Steve

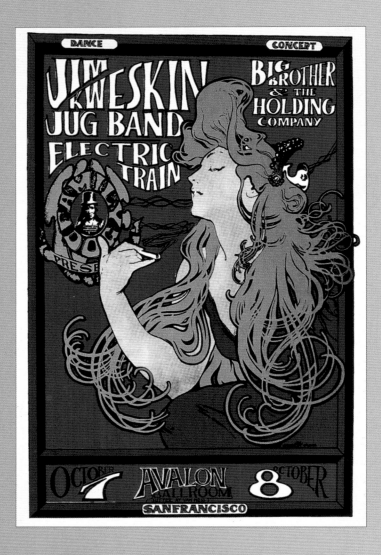

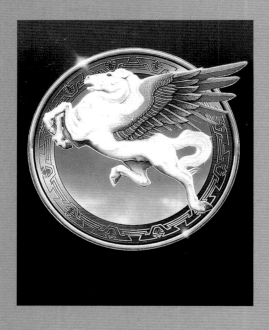

⊙ 'Rajah', Privat
Livemont – 1900

ℭ ℭ Cacao Vanhouten,
lithographic
advertisement, Privat
Livemont – 1899

ℭ 'Job', Alphonse
Mucha – 1898

Miller's *Book Of Dreams* album. Although there clearly appears a direct connection between the two, the modern polished airbrush techniques of Mouse and Kelley places them worlds apart. The lettering on Belle Époque era poster art also lent itself beautifully to the psychedelic poster form, and for this reason has continued to influence many psychedelic artists from the 1960s to the present moment.

↶ Peter Bailey – 1967
BG 59

↷ Closing of
the Fillmore, David
Singer – 1971
BG 287

↺ Rolling Stones
European tour, John
Pasche – 1970

↻ 'Pan', Josef Sattler
– 1895

↺↺ David Singer – 1969
BG 185

Other styles from the past, variously termed "Liberty", "Art Nouveau" and "Jugendstil" launched a complete change in the relationships between images and words in posters. The principle innovators in Europe were Aubrey Beardsley (1872-1898), William Morris (1834-1896), Charles Rennie Mackintosh (1868-1928), Henry van de Velde (1860-1928) and Gustav Klimt (1862-1918). One of the most famous of these posters, influenced by Post Cubism, is the 1927 railway poster by Adolphe Mouron Cassandre, who was born in Crackow, Poland in 1941. Titled 'Nord Express', and executed on behalf of the French Railroads, it displays a train, shortened in a futuristic fashion, while the overhead electric wires provide a sense of motion and great speed. The words, however, form simple captions, as though the Bauhaus had never existed. The Rolling Stones have shown a preference for this style of poster to advertise their world tours, and it therefore provided the inspiration for John Pasche, who designed a number of them for the Stones.

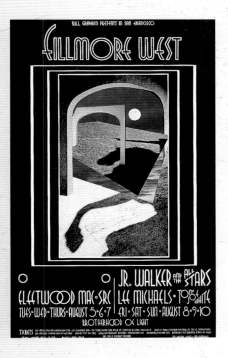

The art of psychedelic poster artist Victor Moscoso may remind us of the work of Henry van de Velde, 1899, with his multiple lines crafting design out of lettering. 'Tropon The Most Concentrated Food', exhibited at the Musée des Arts Decoratifs in Paris, is one such work.

Bonnie MacLean who designed posters for a number of Fillmore West shows, gained inspiration from the swirling lettering and patterns seen in the 1895 work 'Delftshe Slaolie' by Jan Toorop, which is also exhibited in the Musée des Arts Decoratifs. Wes Wilson was another of the psychedelic artists whose work reflected the influence of Jan Toorop.

Mention should be made of two of the greatest poster artists of the Nouveau period, Jules Chéret and Henri Toulouse-Lautrec. Their creations were the forerunners of psychedelic poster art. They were illustrating to create and foster a new ambience outside theatres and on the streets for a viewing public composed of the middle and lower-middle citizens who strolled the boulevards and patronised the theatres and music halls of Paris.

The lettering, and accompanying scenes of gaiety, fun and colour were openly displayed out on the street for passers-by to remark and enjoy, just as pedestrians on the streets of London and San Francisco during the late 1960s could view the psychedelic posters which joyfully informed them that entertainment, excitement and enlightenment were available just around the corner.

To the counterculture of the 1960s, Art Nouveau became a vehicle through which the participants could express their new-found freedoms. Fashions became fluid and flowing, hair was worn long and dresses, such as those designed for Biba by Barbara Hulanicki, imitated early twentieth century styles. Art Nouveau opulence and decadence fitted ideally with the tastes of the Flower Children of the 1960s.

↪ 'Edwardian Ball', Fillmore Auditorium, Stanley Mouse and Alton Kelley – 1966

↻ 'Tropon The Most Concentrated Food', Henry van de Velde – 1899

↺ 'Optical Occlusion', Avalon Ballroom, Joe Gomez – 1967 FD 93

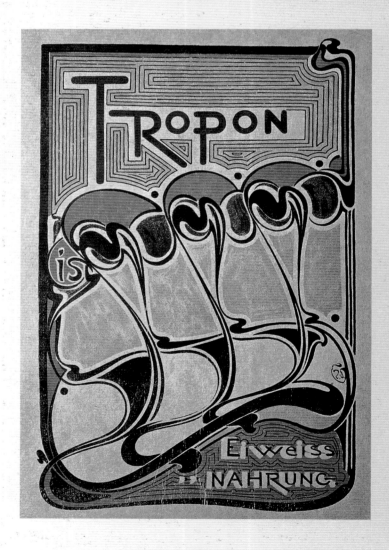

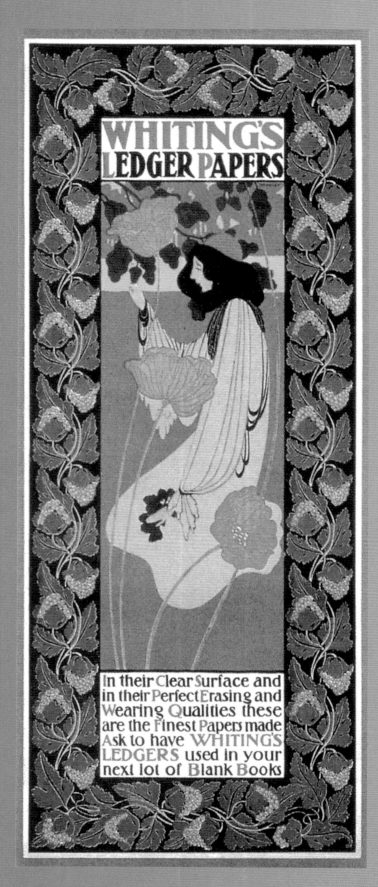

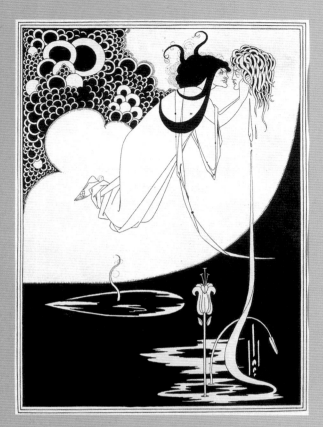

⊙ Illustration from *Salome*, Aubrey Beardsley – 1894

⊘ 'Whiting's Ledger Paper', WH Bradley – 1896

⊍ 'The Kiss', Gustav Klimt – 1907/8

PSYCHEDELIC POSTER - A WORKING DEFINITION

The dictionary definition of what constitutes a "poster" describes "a large, usually printed placard, bill or announcement, often illustrated, that is posted to advertise or publicise something; or an artistic work, often a reproduction of an original painting or photograph, printed on a large sheet of paper."[1] While this generic description includes "psychedelic posters", it does not begin to explain how they differ from that norm.

Academically, it is difficult to truly comprehend the psychedelic poster in the absence of an understanding of the historical and social forces during the development of this unique art form. On the other hand, experientially, (and "experience" is at the essence of the "psychedelic") usually you will know it when you see it. Perhaps the most imaginative and succinct description I have come across was coined by internationally respected poster expert Jacaeber Kastor in his introduction – "Eye Candy" – to the brilliant work *The Art Of The Fillmore*, by Gayle Lemke (Acid Test Productions, 1997).[2]

In 1976, prominent art and cultural historian Walter Medeiros[3] organised the first major museum showing of psychedelic poster art on behalf of the San Francisco Museum of Modern Art. In the catalogue which he prepared for the show, the form was generically described as:

"Earthy, playful, and involving; these works of naive art already contained the rudiments of a definite style. Two stylistic elements are prominent: the commonplace imagery and the dense or 'busy' formats. Psychedelic experience and the light shows made a great impact, and these are the most direct sources, conscious and unconscious, of this element of 'busyness' or visual density. But there are also broader sources for these stylistic qualities. These can only be partially suggested here, but they would include: the impact of popular entertainment, with its value of fun and its visual input, from comics to television; the popularity of collage as a youthful folk art; and the earthy, bohemian aesthetic of randomness and clutter which had been artistically developed in San Francisco's Funk art of the 1950s. Such sources as these combined to create a mental and visual ambience so common and basic to the hippies that it can be seen as the aesthetic sensibility of a unique folk culture. The poster artists were a part of this environment and from their particular backgrounds each expressed it in a different, personal way."

In his introductory essay to *The Art Of The Fillmore*, under a title which also effectively summarised the essence of the psychedelic poster form – "Inside Drawn Out" – Medeiros suggested a series of elements which are uniquely present in psychedelic posters:

"They are handmade – drawn – unlike the 1960s commercial style of photos and typeset lettering. The sheet is fully covered, rich in decorative line and/or pattern. Lettering is compact, shaped into abstract forms, or undulating, stretched or warped. Otherwise, it may be finely rendered and elegantly decorative. Colour is bright, often intense, sometimes with contrasting adjacent hues that cause the edges of form to flicker, flow, or create an illusion of depth. Imagery is often unusual, and unrelated to the event or to the bands on the bill. Images may be sensual, bizarre or beautiful, philosophical or metaphysical."[4]

1: Excerpted from The American Heritage® Dictionary Of The English Language, *Third Edition* © 1996 by Houghton Mifflin Company

2: This work contains invaluable source and reference information. The Art Of The Fillmore *is discussed at greater length in the "Collecting Psychedelic Posters" chapter of this book. The Kastor introduction appears on page 11*

3: Walter Medeiros lived in San Francisco in 1966 and has been a Berkeley resident since 1968. He began studying the San Francisco dance concert posters in 1971 in preparation for a Master's Thesis in Art History (UC Berkeley, 1972). Continued research, writing and lecturing established him as the prominent art and cultural historian of the poster movement. In 1976, as Guest Curator, he organised a retrospective exhibition of the posters at the San Francisco Muse-um of Modern Art. Materials from his Archive of Counter Culture Art were included in The Art Of Rock (Abbeville), Freehand: The Art Of Stanley Mouse (SLG Books), and more recently he wrote an essay for The Art Of The Fillmore (Acid Test Productions)

4: The Medeiros introduction is found in The Art Of The Fill-more, on page 13

🎧 Avalon/Fillmore calendar of forthcoming events, Tom Weller. Photo by John Bailey – 1966

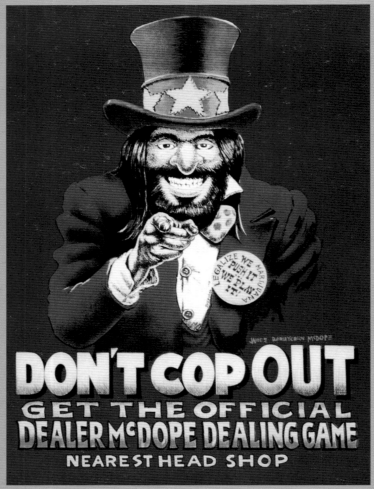

➲ 'Legalise Marijuana',
Dave Sheridan – 1967

↻ Fillmore Auditorium,
Wes Wilson – 1966 BG 9

THE BEATS GO ON

In 1944, a curious meeting of three young men took place at Columbia University in New York City. Almost a decade before the first of their works were published, Allen Ginsberg, Jack Kerouac and William Burroughs came together and began to formulate an expression of culture, based upon expanded consciousness (often with drugs), uncensored self-expression, and unconventional morality. They became the catalyst for the development of the writers, poets, visual artists, filmmakers and musicians who eventually were characterised as the "Beats". It is believed that the term was first used in the late 1940s by a New York City drug addict friend of Burroughs, and was first published in a *New York Times* article in 1952 where the "Beat Generation" was portrayed as "poor, down and out, deadbeat, sad and used". However Kerouac adopted a more upbeat explanation in his 1958 play *The Beat Generation or The New American Church*, asserting that, "Beat means beatitude, not beat up", and, "You feel it in a beat, in jazz – real cool jazz or a good, gutty rock number."

The Beat generation both in America and England was perhaps the most politically involved cultural movement in western history. The Beats became the counterculture advocates of political, spiritual and sexual liberation, welcomed Asian and African American cultures, publicly addressed such previously unmentionable subjects as sex, drugs, censorship and conformity. In so doing, they effectively dismantled many of the pre-existing separations between art and daily life, and spearheaded their own movement that permeated and eventually transformed the prevailing post-war culture.

Jazz music became an important element in the Beat culture. While Ginsberg and Kerouac were still students at Columbia University in New York, Charlie "Bird" Parker and "Dizzy" Gillespie were playing "bebop" or "bop" jazz. Its complex and rapidly changing chords, varied tempos and free improvisation differentiated it from traditional background bar or dance type jazz. On the West Coast, Dave Brubeck, Gerry Mulligan and Chet Baker developed a softer sound of this new form of music called "cool" jazz. Beat writers, including Ginsberg and Kerouac, and San Francisco Beats like Lawrence Ferlinghetti started to organise combined jazz performances and poetry readings, each form complementing and highlighting the other.

However, led by a well-positioned establishment media which was increasingly uncomfortable with their message of individual freedom and responsibility, the Beats were inaccurately depicted as lazy deadbeats who had turned their back on conventional society. Then, after publication and popular success of Allen Ginsberg's *Howl And Other Poems* in 1956, Jack Kerouac's *On The Road* in 1957, and William Burroughs' *Naked Lunch* in 1959, the media appeared to co-opt the new culture by blurring the distinction between the self-described Beats who continued to focus upon personal and artistic growth, and the misleading caricature of what came to be referred to as "Beatniks".

⌒ 'Who Rolled Mary Jane', Stanley Mouse – 1967

➲ 'The Seed', The Charlatans,
Red Dog Saloon, Virginia City,
Nevada. George Hunter and
Michael Ferguson – 1965

↻ Sokol Hall, San Francisco,
Alton Kelley – 1966

The term, first used in print in 1958 by famed *San Francisco Chronicle* columnist Herb Caen, was soon popularised and used to depict a jazz- and poetry-loving hipster wearing black clothing topped by a beret, and carrying around a set of bongo drums. In the face of such now classic 1954 films *The Wild One* and *Rebel Without A Cause*, the messages of Beat authors, artists and musicians became memorialised as mere fashion statements and symbols of rebellion by middle class youth throughout the world. A further proliferation of "Beatnik" characters in television shows and movies, and satire in such publications as *Mad* magazine further trivialised the Beat message. As a result, the stereotype enabled mainstream Americans and British to adopt a non-threatening view of the movement, and to ignore the fact that through their literary and artistic works the Beats continued to aggressively challenge many previously unquestioned societal values and attitudes.

Thus at the dawn of the 1960s, the winds of global societal change were beginning to increase in strength. African Americans were struggling to be accorded the basic human rights which had been promised to them as citizens by the literal words of the American constitution. Their struggle received strong support from many committed women and men of all races, igniting the Civil Rights movement in both North and South. Again, the Beats were in the vanguard of this support effort.

Another major aspect of this social turmoil was the effort of governmental religious leaders to censor expressions of rebellion and freedom, whether in print or on the stage. Lawrence Ferlinghetti, owner of San Francisco's City Lights Bookstore, was arrested and prosecuted for publishing Allen Ginsberg's *Howl*, and other "obscenity" criminal trials were based upon the explicit depictions of homosexual love in *Naked Lunch* by William Burroughs. Fortunately many of these cases produced strong popular verdicts supporting freedom of speech.

SAN FRANCISCO   **It was in June 1965, two years before**
the first "Human Be-In" at San Francisco's Golden Gate Park. The "Summer of Love" really began approximately 150 miles from the Bay Area, when The Charlatans performed their first show at the Red Dog Saloon in Virginia City, Nevada. It proved to be a psychedelic event with

the band fuelled by Augustus Owsley Stanley III's first batch of LSD. The group's romantic cowboy/gambling style image is believed to have been cultivated in direct response to the dapper "mod" style that had come in with the first wave of the British music invasion, led of course by The Beatles.

A poster was designed by Charlatan members George Hunter and Michael Ferguson to advertise the Red Dog events. It became known as "The Seed", and is widely accepted as being the first psychedelic poster of the genre. Distributed hand to hand like a present day "flyer", 'The Seed' became a symbol for this new music, culture and lifestyle, and in the psychedelic hothouse grew into a magnificent flowering of music fusing with art.

➲ 'Western Front Club',
San Francisco, Stanley Mouse – 1967

The Red Dog Saloon fancy dress dances with The Charlatans established a new form of musical event which bore a unique psychedelic identity. After the success of the Red Dog Saloon shows and the new style posters created by Hunter and Ferguson for the occasions, people all over the United States went into motion and began flocking to Virginia City and the West Coast to bathe in the aura of this "new scene".

Also in 1965, another dynamic force for change emerged from the Red Dog Saloon experience. Ellen Harmon, Rock Skully, Bill Ham and Michael Bowen, all one-time tenants of the Pine Street Rooming House in San Francisco, formed the "Family Dog" collective, which under the leadership of third owner Chet Helms would go on to promote San Francisco's musical dominance and fuel the most sensational popular art storm that the world had yet seen. Likewise, in succeeding years Michael Bowen's work as an artist of world-wide repute has been progressively documented in exhibitions, reviews, art periodicals, and in the media in the United States and abroad.

At approximately this same point in time, Bill Graham was working with the San Francisco Mime Troupe, and in the Autumn of 1965, he orchestrated a benefit to aid the Mime Troupe, creating his first flyer to advertise the event. There were three successful "Appeal" shows. Bill built upon that experience to help produce the first LSD "initiation" for the public, the overwhelmingly successful three-night celebration of the "Trips Festival", led by Ken Kesey and the Pranksters held at Longshoreman's Hall in San Francisco on 21-23 January 1966. This three-day Technicolor supernova, a psychedelic scene of apparent chaos and madness, was attended by the cream of Bay Area musicians, attracting film makers, light show and sound technicians, media makers, and of course myriad other creative souls who chose to be included in the experience. Only weeks after this triumph, Bill Graham first opened the doors of the legendary Fillmore Auditorium.

The Family Dog, then under the direction of Ellen Harmon, were also very active in producing psychedelic "initiations" and dances at Longshoreman's Hall in 1965 with such themes as: "Dr Strange – Master of Mysticants", "Sparkle Plenty", and "Ming the Merciless". Family Dog artist Alton Kelley produced the handbills and contributed to the posters for these seminal happenings. Once again The Charlatans were the house band for the Family Dog. In early 1966, they almost single-handedly produced two further shows under the direction of Family Dog partner Luria Castell at the Longshoreman's Hall, designing their own posters for these events as they had done for the Red Dog Saloon.

The psychedelic revolution taking place in San Francisco continued to be fuelled by events produced by Bill Graham, whose shows had attracted many of the old "Beat" crowd, and by performances generated by the Family Dog, led by Chet Helms, who gathered together many of those who fit under the "Prankster" banner. However, all the attendees at these psychedelic dance concerts were really "wild cards". There was an infinite amount of "cross-pollination" between the numerous and varied constituencies which made up the San Francisco Bay Area, including a deluge of newcomers who arrived in the City for the explicit purpose of participating in the scene.

Among the wildest of these "wild cards" were Ken Kesey and his group of psychedelic guerrillas, the Merry Pranksters. Kesey was eager to spread the word about the new wonder drug of fun, LSD, travelling in his battered Day-Glo bus full of Beats, poets, Pranksters and various miscreants, accompanied by his resident band, The Warlocks (soon to become the legendary "Grateful Dead"). Kesey had organised a series of impromptu parties throughout California where he invited the uninitiated to "pass the Acid Test". The handbills to advertise these events are today quite rare and highly collectible.

In San Francisco, the Avalon Ballroom opened under the Family Dog banner, while Bill Graham's Fillmore Auditorium was holding weekly events. Russ Gibb, inspired by the Family Dog, returned to Detroit to open the Grande Ballroom. The success of the Trips Festival, and subsequent events and promotions organised by Bill Graham and Chet Helms, led aspiring promoters throughout America to attempt to open new venues to emulate the success of the San Francisco scene.

So the stage for the vast psychedelic art and music explosion was set, and the identities of many of the leading characters behind all of this new creativity were revealed. We know the broad outline of what they were doing, and we certainly know their music. Our remaining focus will be upon the exciting way in which they ended up advertising themselves and the music, through psychedelic poster art: these eye-catching proclamations nailed to a telephone pole, compelling the innocent bypasser to stop, look, feel and experience.

In the beginning, psychedelic posters and handbills employed simple graphics. Pen ink and pencil were the most economic medium, and most of the art was black design on white or coloured paper. All of this was soon to change, as manifested in the brilliant Bill Graham/Fillmore and the Family Dog/Avalon numbered series posters.

American popular music had been overwhelmed by the British Invasion, led by The Beatles and The Rolling Stones. Just as the early English rock performers had been greatly influenced by unique American music forms such as the Blues, American popular music in the mid 1960s had been moving in a very British direction with look- and sound-alike bands since the early Sixties. Now the time had come for Americans to innovate. Like wildfire, many brilliant, talented bands and musicians came to the fore, including such legendary performers as The Byrds, Big Brother And The Holding Company, Janis Joplin, Jefferson Airplane, Grateful Dead, The Doors, Quicksilver Messenger Service, Country Joe And The Fish and Captain Beefheart and his Magic Band.

The psychedelic rock force was awesome and unstoppable, and the poster artists excelled, each improving weekly while striving to meet the constantly looming deadlines (sometimes overnight) and to match the other's latest effort. The psychedelic West Coast was now calling the shots and the artists, much like the bands they were promoting, stripped away the old and began developing and experimenting with the new.

Left to right: Wes Wilson, Alton Kelley, Stanley Mouse, Victor Moscoso and Rick Griffin
PHOTO: GENE ANTHONY

PROMOTERS AND VENUES

by Walter Medeiros

It all began with the music, of course. In 1965, as part of the English and American rock 'n' roll renaissance, the San Francisco rock bands emerged. With the increasing confidence and ambition of the musicians, and the advent of dance promoters, the San Francisco rock scene grew from informal parties, advertised by word-of-mouth, to large-scale, nationally-famous events. During the high years of 1966 and 1967 dances were regularly presented at numerous halls and clubs, but the Fillmore and the Avalon were the first and most prominent.

Beginning in early 1966, dance concerts were held at these halls from two to five nights per week for several years. The Family Dog organisation, directed by Chet Helms, produced dances at the old Avalon Ballroom until the end of 1968, and at another location for about a year thereafter. During the latter half of 1967 there was also a Family Dog ballroom in Denver, Colorado. The other organisation was directed by Bill Graham, who first regularly produced dances at the Fillmore Auditorium, and later at a larger San Francisco hall called Fillmore West until June 1971. Graham also produced events in other Bay Area auditoriums and in New York City at the Fillmore East. It was through the patronage of these two organisations that the poster developed into a unique, highly creative artform.

◑ 'Blues Rock Bash',
Wes Wilson – 1966 BG 3

◐ 'Baby Jesus', Avalon Ballroom, Wes Wilson – 1966 FD 5

☾ George Hunter of The Charlatans with Mike Wilhelm and Jerry Garcia – 1967
PHOTO: GENE ANTHONY

☾ Chet Helms of the Family Dog and founder of the Avalon Ballroom – 1967
PHOTO: GENE ANTHONY

The uniqueness of the rock poster art derives from two major cultural factors: the special conditions of its patronage and the increasing availability and usage of "dope" (a common catch-all term meaning primarily marijuana and LSD, or "acid"). The music was part of the local "hippie" culture which provided its financial support. ("Hippie" is essentially a neutral and imprecise term. It is used here for its original currency in reference to those people who generally shared the new values of rock music, psychedelic experience, and the accompanying sense of personal freedom and expansion which characterised this segment of the youth movement of the 1960s.)

With such an audience everything was permitted, and the early artists were given almost complete artistic freedom. These posters were liberated from the usual restrictions related to their advertising function. Feeling free, the artists pushed themselves and their art to the limit. Or, more accurately perhaps, the artists returned from their outer limits and put their vision and passion into their art. Suddenly the poster became a very popular artform, the first medium of psychedelic art (excepting light shows), and the leading edge of commercial art. Among the hippies the rock posters were appreciated for their art and also as a matter of identification with the new culture. People took them off the streets and hung them on their walls. The posters were instant art, and they were free.

The Family Dog and the Fillmore produced a total of about 150 and 300 posters respectively, an average of about one per week each. This constitutes the main body of the poster art, but the major artists also produced designs for other dance halls and as art for sale as well. A conservative estimate of all the posters designed by the Fillmore and Family Dog artists alone would come to about 550. Considering that the major ballrooms printed in editions ranging from 300 at first, then 1,500, then 5,000, and that many were later reprinted for retailers, it's apparent that an enormous quantity of high-quality graphic art was produced in San Francisco during the [first] six years of the poster movement.

Like the rock music it served, poster art remains as a record of the consciousness of some of the most perceptive, intelligent and creative youth of the 1960s [and subsequent years]. The viewer who cares to enter into this art, who is willing to invest something of the time, the openness, the imagination, and perhaps the risk which the artists have invested in their work, will come away positively affected by these delightful, beautiful, and sometimes profound works of art. © Walter Medeiros 1976

↻ 'One Year Anniversary', Avalon Ballroom, Alton Kelley and Stanley Mouse – 1966 FD 30

↻↻ 'Tribal Stomp', Wes Wilson: title and photography suggested by Chet Helms – 1966 FD 1

↻ 'Logo', Alton Kelley and Stanley Mouse – 1966 FD 33

↻ 'Sin Dance', Avalon Ballroom, Wes Wilson – 1966 FD 6

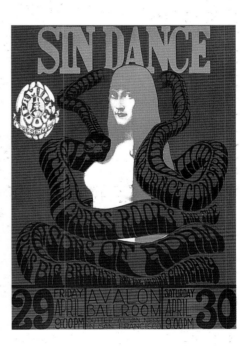

FAMILY DOG – AVALON BALLROOM   In February 1966, Chet Helms, who was managing Big Brother And The Holding Company with Janis Joplin, opened the old Avalon Ballroom at 1268 Sutter Street (at the corner of Van Ness) in San Francisco utilising the Family Dog name and logo. This occurred almost simultaneously with the opening of Bill Graham's Fillmore Auditorium.

Opening night at the Avalon featured The Jefferson Airplane and Big Brother with Janis. The poster produced to advertise this event, designed by artist Wes Wilson, was the first of the Family Dog poster series, bearing the legend FD 1. Many of the posters in this series were referred to not only by their identifying numbers (FD 1 through FD 147), but also by their generic titles; eg 'Skull And Roses' (FD 26), 'Girl With Green Hair' (FD 29), 'Sin Dance' (FD 6).

In addition to the basic Family Dog numbered series, there were posters for Family Dog productions at venues other than the Avalon, including the Great Highway in San Francisco. In late 1967, Chet Helms opened a venue in Denver, Colorado, under the Family Dog banner, and the posters for these shows were numbered FDD 1 through FDD 13. Posters for other non-Avalon shows are generally referred to as the "Family Dog Unnumbered Series".

BILL GRAHAM PRESENTS IN DANCE - CONCERT

JEFFERSON AIRPLANE

QUICKSILVER MESSENGER SERVICE DINO VALENTI FRI SAT SUN FEBRUARY 3 4 5 FILLMORE AUDITORIUM ADM $3.00

Sunday, 2 p.m. - 10 p.m.—Benefit for Berkeley Strike Committee with Jefferson Airplane, Quicksilver Messenger Service, Dino Valenti, Country Joe and the Fish, The Loading Zone, and other friends.

TICKETS SAN FRANCISCO: City Lights Bookstore; The Psychedelic Shop; Bally Lo (Union Square); The Town Squire (1318 Polk); S. F. State College (Hut T-1); Mnasidika. BERKELEY: Discount Records; Shakespeare & Co.; Campus Records. SAN MATEO: Town and Country Records. SAN RAFAEL: Sherman Clay. SAUSALITO: The Tides Bookstore. MENLO PARK: Kepler's Bookstore

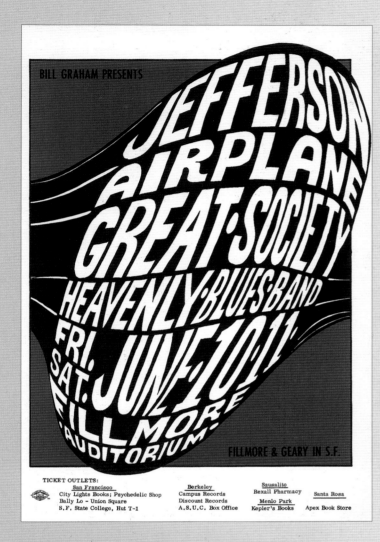

BILL GRAHAM POSTERS

Bill Graham's first posters were used to advertise the San Francisco Mime Troupe events. In 1966 he opened the Fillmore Auditorium, presenting weekly dances and shows featuring the cream of the San Francisco music scene. Posters for these shows comprise the Bill Graham numbered series ("BG-"). The first was drawn to promote the Jefferson Airplane show on 4 February 1996; the last, in June 1971, advertised the closing of the Fillmore show featuring The Grateful Dead, Santana, Quicksilver Messenger Service and Creedence Clearwater Revival.

🎧 Fillmore Auditorium,
Wes Wilson – 1966 BG 10

🎧 Fillmore Auditorium,
Wes Wilson – 1966 BG 17

↪ Bill Graham, Fillmore
Auditorium – 1967
PHOTO: GENE ANTHONY

↩ Fillmore Auditorium,
Wes Wilson – 1967 BG 48

In later years Bill Graham produced concerts at many other venues in the San Francisco Bay Area, advertised by psychedelic posters. These included stadium shows at the Oakland Stadium, Oakland Coliseum, Warfield Theatre, Berkeley Community Theatre, the Greek Amphitheatre at the University of California, Berkeley, and Frost Amphitheatre at Stanford University. In the 1980s, he opened the Shoreline Amphitheatre in Mountain View, approximately thirty miles south of San Francisco, and promoted shows at the Concord Pavilion, located approximately thirty-five miles east of the city.

FILLMORE EAST   The Fillmore East was Bill Graham's foray into the New York City concert scene. Opening in March 1968, and closing in June 1971, many of the most famous groups of the era performed there, including Jimi Hendrix, The Grateful Dead, Jefferson Airplane, Big Brother And The Holding Company (with Janis Joplin), BB King and Buddy Guy. The Who appeared on several occasions with other bands and also presented their seminal rock opera *Tommy* at this venue. The closing show featured The Allman Brothers Band, The J Geils Band and Albert King.

WINTERLAND THEATRE   Winterland Arena in San Francisco became the preferred venue for Bill Graham presentations after the Fillmore was closed in July 1971, hosting shows by such premier groups as The Rolling Stones, The Who, Quicksilver Messenger Service and even The Sex Pistols. Because of its location in the heart of San Francisco, The Grateful Dead adopted the venue for its home fans. Winterland ran for six years, and in 1978 closed to the sounds of the Dead (with opening act The Blues Brothers). Stanley Mouse and Alton Kelley designed the startling 'Blue Rose' poster for this New Year's Eve show.

↶ Fillmore East, New York, David Byrd – 1967

↷ 'Christmas Show', Winterland, Gut – 1967

Winterland
PHOTO: GENE ANTHONY

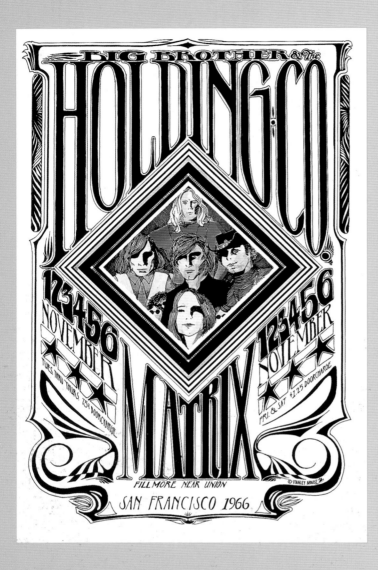

☾ Big Brother
And The Holding
Company,
the Matrix,
San Francisco,
Stanley Mouse – 1966
(original artwork)

➲ Kaleidoscope
Club, Hollywood,
Dahlgren – 1968

☋ Kaleidoscope
Club, Hollywood,
Farmer – 1967

THE MATRIX In 1965, Marty Balin, musician and co-founder of The Jefferson Airplane, opened the Matrix Club at 3138 Fillmore Street in San Francisco. Promoting acts which included Lightnin' Hopkins, Steve Miller, Quicksilver Messenger Service and Big Brother And The Holding Company, the Matrix acted as a showcase for emerging as well as established talents.

The early posters produced for the Matrix were created by Heinrich Kley, Mark T Berens and Leidenthal leading to Victor Moscoso's stunning 'Neon Rose' series, and also including Stanley "Mouse" Miller's mighty November 1966 poster for a show with Big Brother And The Holding Company.

The Moscoso series in early 1967 featured unusual colour combinations which made them difficult to read (although easier when under the influence of various mind-altering substances), but always hypnotic and visually engrossing.

LOS ANGELES KALEIDOSCOPE The Kaleidoscope Club at 1228 Vine Street (near Hollywood Boulevard) was originally the location of the Earl Carroll Theatre. It featured a round, revolving stage. The posters designed for concerts and shows at the Kaleidoscope were consequently circular and approximately the size of a ten inch LP. These posters were unique, and believed to be the only circular psychedelic posters produced during the era. The poster artists who designed for the Kaleidoscope included Dahlgren, Mortimer, Lanning Stern and Farmer.

PINNACLE PRODUCTIONS AT THE SHRINE AUDITORIUM   **Pinnacle Productions was established by Los Angeles artist**
John van Hamersveld, who had grown up on Los Angeles
area beaches with fellow surfer Rick Griffin (later to become among the most famous of the American psychedelic poster artists).
Van Hamersveld organised and motivated the Los Angeles hip community, and pioneered the first Los Angeles psychedelic dances.

Influenced by the San Francisco shows, and the work of Griffin and Mouse, he promoted his
events primarily at the Shrine Auditorium. Initially, he designed and printed the posters for the
Shrine shows by himself, the first of which took place in 1967, and featured stunning graphics.

Later, in 1968, he farmed out the poster work to Rick Griffin, Victor Moscoso and other poster
artists. The most famous posters from this venue are 'Amazing Electric Wonders' and 'Indian', which
are highly collectible. Van Hamersveld has since designed more than 300 album covers and the 365
foot long mural for the 1984 Los Angeles Olympic Games.

☾ 'Indian', Shrine
Auditorium, John van
Hamersveld – 1967

☽ Shrine Auditorium,
Los Angeles, Victor
Moscoso – 1968

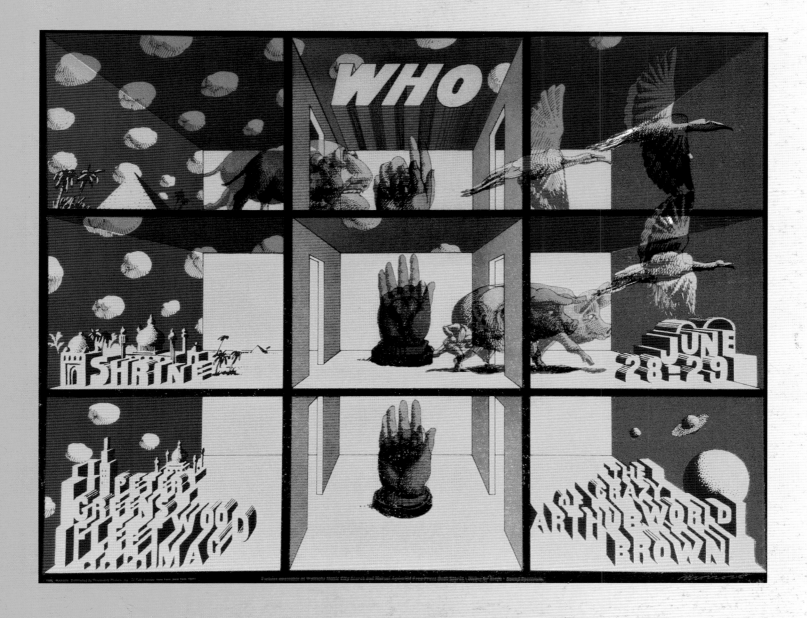

© 1966, 1993 GARY GRIMSHAW   Printed by GHETTO PRESS · Detroit   6/325 Gary Grimshaw

GRANDE BALLROOM – DETROIT: RUSS GIBB PRESENTS

Russ Gibb, inspired by the Family Dog concerts and the San Francisco scene, returned to his home town of Detroit in late 1966 determined to promote his versions of Family Dog type events. He presented the new wave of local psychedelic bands, The MC5 being the most popular.

Subsequently, the "heavyweight bands" of the era, including The Jefferson Airplane, Grateful Dead, Cream, Jimi Hendrix and The Byrds came to Detroit to play at Russ Gibb's "Grande Ballroom". The posters to promote the Grande Ballroom events were created by a new group of artists: Gary Grimshaw and Carl Lundgen, whose work would soon rival that of the San Francisco artists, ranking them also at the top of the psychedelic poster genre.

Because of the limited budget of the Grande, more handbills than posters were produced to advertise the events. However the artwork equalled that of the San Francisco artists in quality and creativity.

↻ 'Seagull',
Grande Ballroom,
Detroit, Gary Grimshaw
– 1966

↺ Grande Ballroom,
Detroit, Gary Grimshaw
– 1967

POSTER ARTISTS : WES WILSON

by Walter Medeiros

Contact Printing was a small San Francisco press located in proprietor Bob Carr's basement. Carr was in contact with the San Francisco jazz, poetry and art scene and his low-budget operation brought him jobs such as the production of the Mime Troupe handbills. As an assistant, Carr took on a somewhat younger friend, Wes Wilson, who had some artistic skill and an interest in printing. Wilson did the layout and design and Contact's reputation for quality and economy eventually resulted in commissions from the new music promoters. These handbills established Wilson as a poster designer, and when the dance concerts became weekly events at the Fillmore and Avalon ballrooms, both Chet Helms and Bill Graham relied on Wilson for poster designs.

Wilson was concerned with design and form and examination of his work shows his consistent development, from his early experiments to the eventual masterworks of drawing, design and colour. With his first full-size poster Wilson changed his design approach from the tight compositions of his handbills to the more flexible and expressive technique of freehand lettering. This design resembles the early handbills, especially 'The Seed', with its density of format and variety of capricious lettering. But the letter shapes are his own and the full format derives from his own approach to drawing, which was to "fill up space", rather than placing an isolated object on a bare sheet.

Besides filling up space, Wilson wanted to make the poster expressive of the printing process. He approached the design as in wood block printing, in which portions of the printing surface are cut away to obtain the desired form. This was achieved by outlining the letters and inking in between them, leaving the letters to emerge as white "negative" space. Wilson often used lettering as a background for a three-dimensional image and this lettering method, and the use of flowing, non-uniform shapes provided a quick and easy way to lay out the lettering in the irregular, leftover spaces around the figure.

Wilson mastered these techniques with his third poster, which is one of his strongest early designs.

The early dances were high-energy, good-time events. This happened quite naturally, but Chet Helms, the Family Dog director, was a cultural activist and he generally sought to enhance or focus the energy. To this end he often provided themes for the dances and relevant images, titles, and phrases to be included in the posters. These images and titles expressed his funky humour and carried the general message "loosen up, have a ball, dance your blues away, break on through!" The image of the madcap dancers is a perfect symbol of the energetic abandon which characterised the early dances. The imagery and titles of the 'Euphoria', 'The Laugh Cure' and 'Hupmobile 8' posters are other examples of Helms' "off-the-wall" humour.

↪ Grateful Dead,
Fillmore Auditorium,
Wes Wilson – 1967 BG 51

↩↪ The Association,
Fillmore Auditorium,
Wes Wilson – 1966 BG 18

↪ Quicksilver
Messenger Service,
Fillmore Auditorium,
Wes Wilson – 1966 BG 7

↻ New Generation,
Fillmore Auditorium,
Wes Wilson – 1966 BG 6

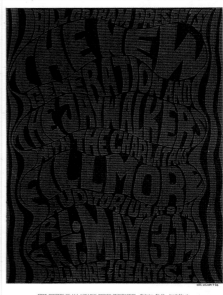

BILL GRAHAM PRESENTS IN SAN FRANCISCO

WES WILSON ©1967 BILL GRAHAM -51- PRINTED BY WEST COAST LITHO GRAPH CO.

☭ The Blues Project,
Fillmore Auditorium,
Wes Wilson – 1967 BG 50

☭☭ The Grateful Dead,
Fillmore Auditorium,
Wes Wilson – 1967 BG 45

At the same time Wilson was also producing posters for Bill Graham, and the workload eventually became too great. During these first months, Wilson had produced his strongest posters under the influence of the Family Dog, but given the choice of which client to drop, he took the path of artistic freedom since Graham gave him essentially free rein. Given this ideal condition, Wilson pursued his own direction, which consisted of experimenting with the integration of lettering and form. Wilson has a strong humanist orientation and the head and the human figure are favourite images. The full figure would come later; in his early work he restricted himself to various experiments with the simpler form of the head. At first he simply fitted the lettering into a head shape. Later, for the 'Mindbenders' poster he was able to create an abstract design which expressed what the music was likely to do to your grey matter.

Wilson also created a variety of abstract forms with his lettering, and these are all rounded and somewhat organic. These shapes derive from his basic form preference and from various dance environment sources, such as the colourful splashes of the liquid projection light shows. Wilson was also working toward expression with colour and in one of his early designs he attempted to reproduce certain vertical flowing effects which he had experienced on LSD. The result fell short of his intent but for the first time colour, form and dense pattern were consciously exploited to express psychedelic vision. Wilson continued to pursue this problem and after several experiments with colour and lettering it all came together in the sensational 'Red Flames' design. For its synthesis of form and colour into a unique work of psychedelic art this poster stood out like a beacon. Except for a few of Wilson's later posters, nothing came close to such compact intensity until half a year later.

Certain rock posters display a similarity to the style of Art Nouveau and it has been implied that the San Francisco artists are greatly indebted to that style. Research and systematic examination of the posters indicate that, in fact, Art Nouveau had no formative influence upon rock poster art. The early poster artists were not academically trained; they were do-it-yourself amateurs, generally unaware of art history and very much into their "own thing". 'The Seed' contains a bit of the vegetal-floral motif so typical of Art Nouveau, but it was not this stylistic element that was influential. The origins of the rock poster style are in the patterns, colour and flowing forms of psychedelic vision/experience, and in the commonplace Victorian-style graphics and artefacts of the American West. Only later, when the posters had attained their basic style, did some of the artists adopt elements from Art Nouveau, and even then only rarely.

This is especially relevant to Wilson's art, particularly his lettering. Wilson was uninterested in and unaware of art styles of the past. His style developed out of his own specific approach to art and poster making, qualified by such influences as psychedelic experience and the psychedelic art of the light shows. About the time of the 'Red Flames' design, however, an acquaintance showed Wilson a reproduction of a 1908 poster by Alfred Roller, an artist of the Viennese Secessionist movement. The lettering resembled Wilson's, and though he had never seen such lettering, he recognised it as the direction in which he had been working. It was a more crisp and elegant form of his own method of dealing with letters and words as blocks of form and he readily incorporated Roller's style into his art.

As to basic design, the vast majority of Wilson's posters contain rounded, sculptural forms. Now and then, however, he returned to explore the flat "architectural" format. This is not an original poster format but Wilson handled it distinctively, and it's a reflection of his specific interest in architecture and his strong orientation toward orderly, systematic modes. He experimented with abstract, decorative patterns in these and also enlivened several with "hot" colour. In a variation of this format he again explored the flame motif, this time breaking it down into flickering little strokes that recall the brushwork of Van Gogh.

☞ 'The Quick And The Dead', Avalon Ballroom, Wes Wilson – 1966 FD 12

☞ Captain Beefheart, Fillmore Auditorium, Wes Wilson – 1966 BG 34

As soon as Wilson had mastered his techniques of design and lettering, he tamed his attention to drawing, and the predominant image of his later work is that of "woman". This is not in itself surprising; woman is a traditional subject of art, and sensuality and sexual freedom were prominent aspects of the hippie culture. But for thoughtful people sexuality has deeper symbolic dimensions as well. Although sensuality is present and sometimes openly celebrated in Wilson's art, his frequent portrayal of the female figure is not essentially about woman as a sex object.

His first two female images took the form of the full-figure nude. In subsequent drawings the women expressed a more serious, spiritual quality. These were usually partial figures, with bodies swathed in drapery or formed of lettering or abstract decorative pattern, and with the focus upon the head. Several of these women images are associated with a symbol, most often the yin-yang, and they all confront the viewer with a calm, serious expression. They appear as priestesses of some sort, keepers of some inner wisdom. The religious-philosophical context – a subject of serious interest to Wilson – is sometimes directly evoked through costume.

Other figures, through association with the yin-yang symbol or a design such as the 'Tree Of Life', conjure impressions of "duality", "union of opposites", and the feminine role of life-bearer. These images transcend their specific forms to become symbolic of universal principles.

In Christian art there is the symbol of the skull, an injunction to "remember death". In Wilson's equally serious, but more optimistic art, it is as though the anonymous skull has been given female flesh and looks out at us in different guises, but always evocative of the principle of life. The female figure as life symbol is, of course, older than art, but this unique quality of Wilson's sensual/spiritual figures places them in a category of the most serious, positive use of the female image in recent times.

Wilson occasionally returned to drawing the full-figure nude. One of these depicts a woman with a snake, the classic symbol of disharmony in the male-female relationship. This image was soon followed by the lovely 'Golden Lady' who appears as the embodiment of female perfection. She projects openness, modesty, intelligence and calm inner strength – her beauty radiates from within. She is Venus, Madonna and Earth Mother.

The lettering of the 'Golden Lady' poster is perhaps Wilson's most unreadable. The unreadability of these posters was not a matter of studied intent, it simply evolved from Wilson's form and pattern-making approach and as a graphic expression of psychedelic vision. These posters were intended for a very special audience, one whose sensibilities were also informed by psychedelic experience, and far from resenting the lack of clarity, they welcomed the intense visual trips which the posters provided. Bill Graham sometimes complained about legibility but nevertheless continued to grant the artistic freedom which was a critical factor in the development of these unique works of commercial art.

🎧 Jefferson Airplane, Winterland and Fillmore Auditorium, Wes Wilson – 1967 BG 54

☾ The Byrds, Winterland and Fillmore Auditorium, Wes Wilson – 1967 BG 57

☾ Grateful Dead, Fillmore Auditorium, Wes Wilson – 1966 BG 41

Multiple merging figures appear in many of Wilson's posters, especially those of his last few months of production. These drawings are partially derived from LSD perceptions, either from personal self-encounter or from other vivid experiences such as the "feeling-knowledge" about the unity and continuity of life which occurred to most people who "dropped acid". The artists seldom attempted to draw while "stoned" but they brought back strong impressions which sometime later emerged in their art. This is especially true of Wilson, whose approach to art was to draw the realities of his own time and his own being. The poster artists acknowledged the full spectrum of reality, and as Wilson matured artistically he sometimes openly expressed the disharmonies of his internal and external life. He had no reluctance about exposing such feelings, nor doubts about the acceptance of such poster art. People saw the art in their own way, and he knew that all kinds of heaviness was going on out there.

The expression of movement, of lateral or upward flow of form was a graphic achievement which Wilson intermittently pursued from his earliest works. Among his last posters are two drawings that are expressive of duality and life-energy flow. These are among the most dynamic of Wilson's designs. They are examples of the artist at his best, his mind and hand at ease, together, and freely flowing. Great plasticity of form and space are created with very simple means and the central figures create an upward-spiralling movement that returns on itself and leads the eye again and again on its winding, inward path.

The ancient, dynamic cycle of life, the duality of opposites involved in its transmission, in Wilson's art, especially his later drawings, such content is masterfully integrated into powerful graphic form. LSD was a modern firebrand. It could burn you out or light your way. For the strong and thoughtful it opened up new awareness and old knowledge – of the self and of Life. With it came, for many people at least, great expectations, a strong sense of new and bright beginnings. Knowledge was embraced as an essential factor of personal and social development. In his flowing design for the Levi Strauss retirement party poster Wilson expressed to the older generation this new, yet ancient hope for an upward-spiralling Golden Age: "We dream of a time when knowledge comes of age to show us a beginning which has no ending." © *Walter Medeiros 1976*

☾ Moby Grape,
Winterland and
Fillmore Auditorium,
Wes Wilson – 1967 BG 56

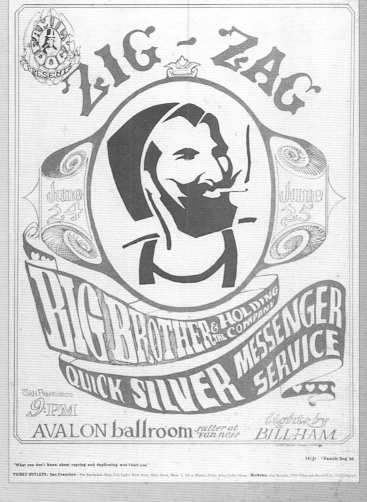

➲ 'Zig-Zag',
Avalon Ballroom, Stanley Mouse
and Alton Kelley – 1966 FD 14

↻ 'Redskin', Youngbloods,
Avalon Ballroom, Stanley Mouse
and Alton Kelley – 1966 FD 39

↻ Stanley Mouse at 710 Ashbury
PHOTO: GENE ANTHONY

STANLEY MOUSE
& ALTON KELLEY

by Walter Medeiros

Alton Kelley had been a member of the original Family Dog and had designed the handbills for their first dances. Kelley was not an established artist or a printer and was in no position to produce posters for Helms when Helms began producing dances. In early 1966 Kelley met Stanley "Mouse" Miller, and when Wes Wilson quit in June they took over the poster production, working under the name "Mouse Studios".

A funky, off-the-wall art style came naturally to Kelley and Mouse. Both were high-spirited, active rock 'n' roll "street kids" involved in activities around custom cars and motorcycles since their teens. Kelley grew up in the New England area. As a young man he briefly attended an art school but didn't take it seriously and left to work as an auto and aircraft mechanic. Later he moved to Los Angeles where he worked in a motorcycle shop and raced motorcycles on weekends.

Mouse came from Detroit. His father was an artist and a sign painter. He had been drawing since childhood and was nicknamed "Mouse" in high school as a result of his numerous cartoons involving Mickey Mouse. In the mid 1950s he was

painting flames and "pinstriping" on custom cars and airbrushing hot rods and monsters on T-shirts at custom car shows. This experience was formative; it accounts for his basic skill with the decorative lettering and flowing linework that is characteristic of his poster art.

In addition to their art, these unusually compatible partners had an important influence on the poster scene. The friendly, easygoing attitude which permitted their mutual collaboration later fostered a spirit of collaboration among other Family Dog artists. They enjoyed sharing the high of poster making, and "jams" sometimes occurred when several of these artists were "hanging out" and working together in somebody's kitchen table "studio". Under a cloud of smoke, ideas and energy escalated and they sometimes worked on one another's designs. Also, Mouse Studios' graphic style set a standard which inspired two other prominent poster artists, Rick Griffin and Randy Tuten.

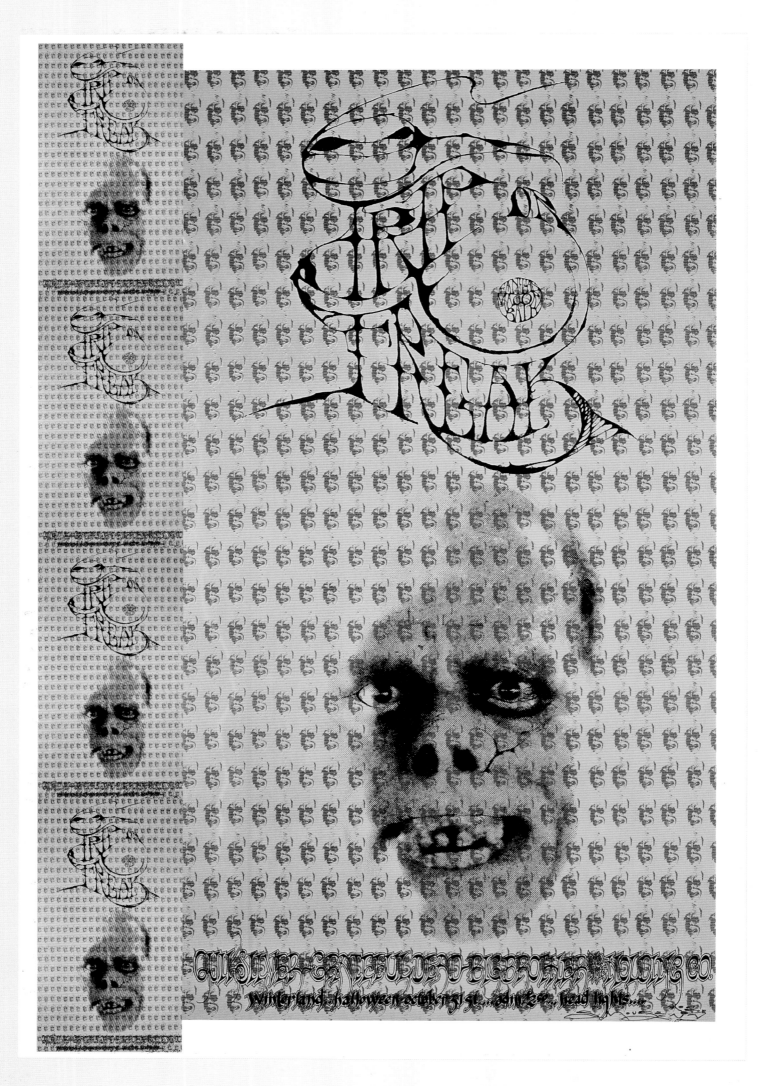

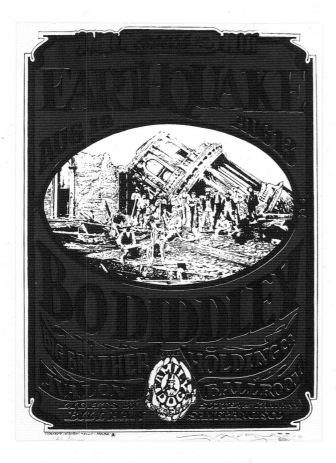

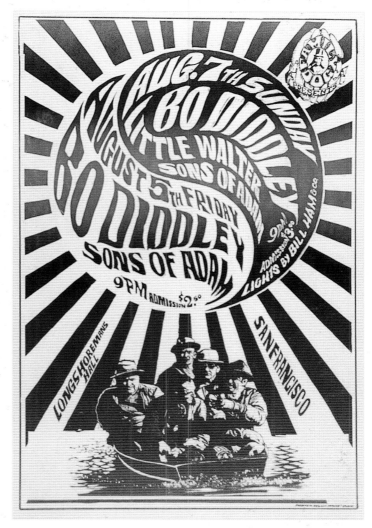

🎧 'Earthquake', Avalon
Ballroom, Alton Kelley
and Stanley Mouse
– 1966 FD 21

⟳ 'Men In A Rowboat',
Longshoreman's Hall,
Alton Kelley and Stanley
Mouse – 1966 FD 20

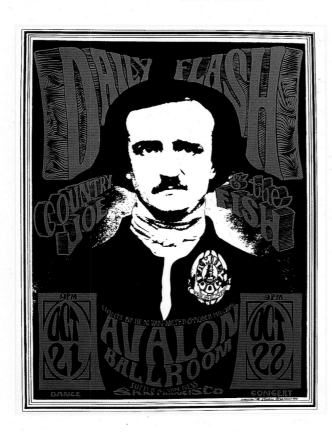

Kelley and Mouse shared equally in the design and production
of their posters, but since Kelley was not yet a skilled draftsman,
it is Mouse's hand that is most apparent in their work. Kelley's
special medium was collage; he had been making collages with
images cut from magazines since his high school days. Collage
was used very little in their rock posters, but Kelley's skill
with this medium can be seen in his 'Joint Show' poster and
in two collaborations with Griffin.

Kelley and Mouse were keenly
aware of the power of images. Their
approach was that of traditional poster
designers but much freer and more
daring. They worked on the assumption
that the primary function of a poster is
to attract attention and they achieved it
with a strong image, either one they
created or one they found. Typically,

⟳ 'Edgar Allan Poe',
Daily Flash, Avalon Ball-
room, Stanley Mouse and
Alton Kelley – 1966 FD 31

⟳⟳ 'Trip Or Freak',
Winterland, poster and
handbills, Stanley
Mouse, Alton Kelley
and Rick Griffin – 1967

their art exploits the "attraction power" of recognisable
images. Their first several posters revived the advertising style,
primarily through the use of product label formats. Also, they
had a healthy sense of irreverence toward narrow proprietary
values and sufficient self-confidence to be outrageous, and on

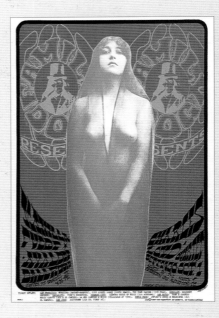

↶ 'Dian', Vanilla Fudge,
Avalon Ballroom,
Alton Kelley – 1967 FD 85

↷↷ 'Wolf', Howlin' Wolf,
Avalon Ballroom,
Alton Kelley and Stanley
Mouse – 1966 FD 27

↷ 'Skull And Roses',
Grateful Dead,
Avalon Ballroom,
Alton Kelley and Stanley
Mouse – 1966 FD 26

some of these posters they used certain famous trademarks. In their most daring and effective poster of this type they exploited the special attraction power (for the hippies) of the label of the Zig-Zag cigarette rolling papers.

Such use of established images was not a matter of plagiarism or poverty of imagination. An attitude of openness and freedom was the most prominent characteristic of the hippie culture, and visually, Kelley and Mouse were in the vanguard. They are of the age of media with its heavy dosage of visual input, especially from television. For them, all images were part of a common visual vocabulary and dope reaffirmed that everything is everything. Complete originality was no longer an absolute criterion for art. "Found art" had long since made it in the art world in the form of assemblage and collage. Kelley and Mouse worked with images found in the entertainment world, commerce, art – anything that fitted. They never used images in a "put down" way. They always used them, it might be said, with love.

These trademarks and other commonplace images were used to create a "flash" on something that would turn people on; a "hit" of fun, beauty, or something otherwise impressive.

Often there are references to experiences common to their peers. In the early days of the hippie scene it was a hit to see the Zig-Zag man in public, or a stoned "Smokey the Bear" holding his "axe" with "Smoke!" on his belt buckle. Cultural references were usually more general, however. Sometimes the image was used simply for its inherent reference, such as the wrapper of the Abba Zaba candy bar, which was popular in California, and the motorcycle with the auto engine labelled "Truth".

More often the images were used satirically or in some other new context. Half-wit Alfred E Neuman of *Mad* magazine appears amid puns derived from the band name "Other Half"; the collage in the 'Buffalo Springfield' poster satirises the massive sound systems which some rock bands used; and the inherently powerful photo of a "contour-mapped" head also contains psychedelic implications. In addition to a powerful image, Kelley and Mouse wanted every poster to look different. In contrast to Wilson's art, development of form or ideas is not a relevant aspect of their work. Except for some minor details of style and technique, almost any design could have been produced at any other time. A few themes can be found, however, and though it is more relevant to consider each poster as an independent piece, these groupings can serve to focus on some of the qualities and sources of their art. As to content, the broad theme of funky or commonplace images is the most distinctive and applicable. Within this there are two minor categories, Indians and women.

Indians were a popular subject with the hippies; their earthy and communal lifestyle was appreciated, and the hippies' "outsider" feelings early on took the form of tribal identification. The long hair, costume and many other things about Indians were also appreciated. Depending upon individual personality,

GRATEFUL DEAD

SEPT 16 · SEPT 17

THE OXFORD CIRCLE
SUTTER AT VAN NESS S.F.
AVALON BALLROOM

TICKET OUTLETS: *SAN FRANCISCO* THE PSYCHEDELIC SHOP; CITY LIGHTS BOOKS; BALLY LO; CEDAR ALLEY COFFEE HOUSE; MNASIDIKA; DISCOUNT RECORDS (North Beach); SANDAL MAKER (North Beach) · *SAUSALITO* *BERKELEY* *MENLO PARK* · TIDES BOOK SHOP; SANDAL MAKER RECORD CITY, 234 Telegraph Avenue KEPLER'S BOOK STORE

the understanding of and identification with Indians ranged from the profound and serious to the fashionable and trivial. But at every level of identification there was a positive attitude toward them. The Indian was an image of dignity and strength and without exception this respect was projected in the poster art.

Kelley and Mouse designed about a half-dozen Indian posters, most of which used photos or existing artwork. Their most powerful design is their portrayal of Chingachgook, the fearsome warrior-scout of JF Cooper's early nineteenth century novel *The Last Of The Mohicans*. This poster is simply a celebration of that classic Indian character. He projects powerfully from the oval frame, just as in the novel he looms ominously as "a terrific emblem of death, drawn (in his war paint) in intermingled colours of white and black". The dynamic power of the image is carried out in the asymmetrical format, the colour, the angular patterns, and the use of the swastika, which is here restored to its proper place as a universal symbol of ancient cultures.

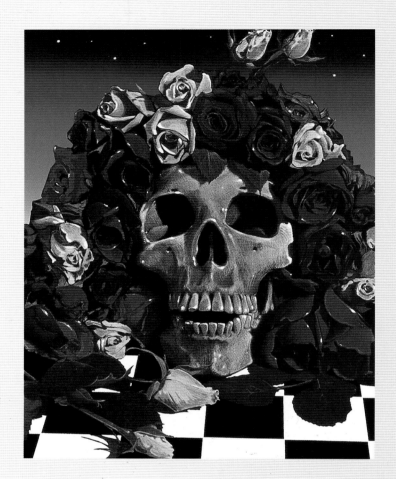

↻ 'Timeless',
Stanley Mouse

↻ 'Rose Photographer',
book cover for Grateful
Dead Family Album,
Stanley Mouse

The number of female images is only slightly larger than that of Indians. They sometimes resorted to this subject when they couldn't think of what else to do in a hurry, but they never used modern sex queens. They often chose an old vamp photo, when sex was veiled and mysterious, or an image that was more sedate and simply beautiful.

Except for these themes, the only other category to be found in their art consists of those designs which may be called classic, either for stylistic reasons or in the sense of being the highest standard, a model of its kind. It is perhaps rather surprising to find that the term "classical" – in the stylistic sense – is applicable to this hippie art, especially to that of this irreverent pair. As with most movements, it is the new and the exotic, which usually attracts the first and most attention. In many ways Kelley and Mouse were innovative and quite unconventional. But their technical interests and their values of clarity and variety taught them respect for traditional, orderly modes as well, and some of their later designs are composed with classic simplicity, balance, and restraint, such as the 'Cosmic Collage'; the sedate, handsome 'Plaque', and many others.

Traditionally, the entertainment poster contains visual identification of the performers. This is usually done with a photograph, but with the rock groups their names and character often provided imaginative artists an opportunity for metaphor and symbolism. The Grateful Dead were perhaps the earliest and heaviest music "tribe" in the San Francisco area. In the

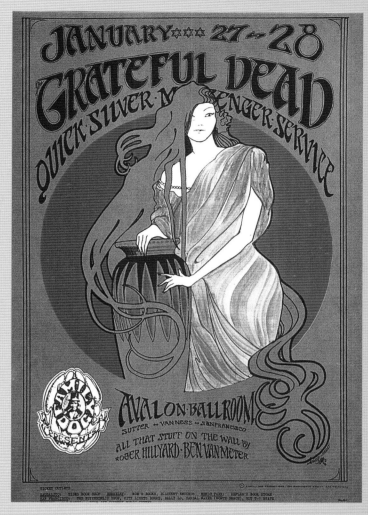

early 1960s they were involved in the LSD happenings initiated by Ken Kesey and his tribe of Merry Pranksters. The Dead got into playing weird, far-out music related to psychedelic trips. Their reputation for such musical excursions, plus their heavy name, led to the eventual adoption of the skull or skeleton as their symbol. It had been used once on an earlier poster, but Mouse Studios' classic 'Skeleton And Roses' design established it as the emblem of The Dead. The figure is EJ Sullivan's illustration for the twenty-sixth quatrain of *The Rubaiyvat*. To see it in the poster is to realise how the artists have enhanced its power through the application of colour, a strong border, and an appropriate graphic style.

⊙ **'Girl With Long Hair', Avalon Ballroom, Stanley Mouse and Alton Kelley – 1967** FD 45

⊙ **'New Year's', Avalon Ballroom, Stanley Mouse and Alton Kelley – 1966** FD 41

Formal order, balance, eternal themes – that's all very well, but those are words and concepts. But the way old Winnie-the-Pooh and Piglet grab you by your childhood heart – that's how you know it's a classic. What a delightful hit from our innocent years. But wait, what's Pooh Bear holding? And my, my, is Piglet smoking?!

Commercial art has its basic functional requirements, which Mouse fully accepts. The rock poster movement was a godsend. It allowed him to explore and develop aspects of his fine art aspirations – which since the late 1970s he has pursued directly in his paintings. Accustomed to the liberation of self-employment, like a fine artist he was always intolerant of arbitrary constraints. For Mouse, the satisfactions of the free artist were especially realised in his experience with frictionless airbrush drawing. After painting for a day or two at a car show, he could slip into a rare groove, a kinetic-aesthetic high. His hand moved unconsciously – swinging laterally, curving, closing in, pulling back – dancing out the appropriate line quality. And the shirt on the easel virtually disappeared: "It was like there was no surface," he recalls. "It was so free-flowing, it was actually thrilling to experience that. I could tell sometimes – 'There it goes, there goes the surface! Whissht, it's gone!' – and then I'd be flying." Such moments were worth a lot but, recalling all the years, and the many fine products of his independent hand, Mouse disclosed his greater achievement: "I had to follow my own direction, and somehow it all worked out. I managed to do what I really wanted." © *Walter Medeiros 1976.*

Mouse has completed numerous commissions since the 1971 re-opening of Mouse Studios: several LP covers for The Grateful Dead, *Mars Hotel* in 1974, *Terrapin Station* in 1976, inventing such characters as "Ice Cream Kid" and "Rainbow Foot".

His prolific output from the 1970s to the present day has also included such memorable pieces as his 'Pegasus' design for the Steve Miller *Book Of Dreams* LP. He continued to collaborate with Kelley and other poster artists, including Randy Tuten. In 1988, he and Rick Griffin completed their masterwork 'Flaming Guitar' painting of Jimi Hendrix. Mouse has published several books featuring his work, and continues to create new artwork at an outstanding pace. His present studio in Sonoma is filled with examples of prolific past work and his equally exciting current posters and paintings. He has continued to accomplish what he really wanted.

➲ **Gathering Of The Tribes, 'Human Be-In', Michael Bowen and Stanley Mouse – 1967**

➲➲ **'Human Be-In', Golden Gate Park. Artists: Michael Bowen, Stanley Mouse and Alton Kelley. Photo: Casey Sonnabend – 1967**

↻ **'Space Man', Avalon Ballroom, Alton Kelley and Stanley Mouse – 1966** FD 28

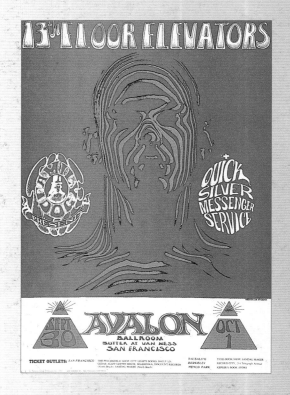

↻ 'Flower Pot',
Blue Cheer, Avalon
Ballroom, Victor
Moscoso – 1967 FD 86

↻ 'Neon Rose',
Poster Show
Exhibition, Dallas,
Victor Moscoso – 1967

VICTOR MOSCOSO

by Walter Medeiros

Victor Moscoso was the first academically trained and experienced graphic artist to join the poster movement. He had studied art at Cooper Union in New York City and at Yale University. In the early 1960s he attended the San Francisco Art Institute where he completed the master's programme in painting; he later remained in San Francisco working as a commercial graphic artist. Moscoso began designing for the Family Dog in the late autumn of 1966 and continued for about a year, during which time commissions were also given to Mouse Studios, Rick Griffin, and later Bob Fried.

Moscoso's first few posters are clearly experimental; he tried various approaches, sometimes adapting elements of Wilson's or Mouse's style to his own purpose. He soon began to find his own way, however, which lay in the direction of visual intensity obtained through optical effects of form and colour. He recalled his intensive colour training with Josef Albers at Yale and also realised that "hot" colour was a way to "load up the surface", that is, to intensify the graphic images and patterns by adding strong colour effects. With a series of brilliantly successful posters for the Matrix, a local [San Francisco] blues and rock music club, he explored the potential of colour combinations which make the edges of form appear to jump or vibrate. These effects brought a

new level of visual intensity to the poster art. The vivid effects of hot colour were inspired by more than just straight artistic perception, of course, but Moscoso never depicted dope directly nor often sought to evoke its mental effects as other artists sometimes did. Rather, he took psychedelic consciousness simply as a matter-of-fact background reality that informed the creation of graphic art.

Astrological references can be seen in several of Moscoso's designs. The Family Dog art director was involved in astrology and would sometimes provide Moscoso with information and themes related to the planetary conjunctions on the day of the event. Dance titles and themes were a tradition

↻ The Matrix,
Victor Moscoso, Neon
Rose Series – 1967

↻ 'Sphinx Dance', Steve Miller
Blues Band, Avalon Ballroom,
Victor Moscoso – 1967 FD 47

↻ 'Horns Of Plenty', Quicksilver
Messenger Service, Avalon Ballroom,
Victor Moscoso – 1967 FD 68

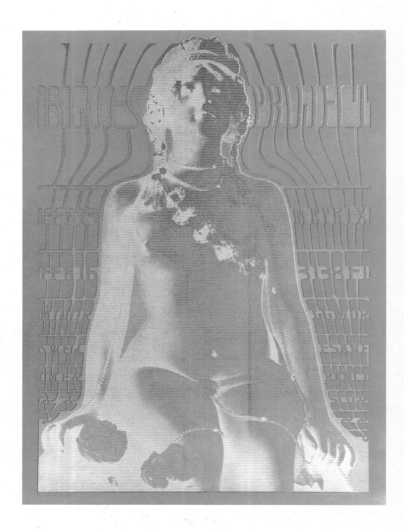

at the Family Dog, and if Moscoso liked the idea and had nothing else in mind, he incorporated the astrological information into his design. Those who took such matters seriously may have read heavy messages in this astrological content but the artist intended nothing more than to create a design with these given elements of a popular subject.

Moscoso was the first artist to use photo-collage and he exploited its potential for surrealism. He produced only a half-dozen such collage designs, most of which had colour effects happening within them. This format was useful for quick, overnight jobs. Most of the design time was spent on the collage, which was then inserted into the relatively simple, but precisely executed frame. Application of a hot colour scheme resulted in what Moscoso calls a "vibrating border".

During his later "decorative pattern" period, Moscoso produced an unusual collage design on the theme of the dance. The realistic silhouettes of the couple give them life – we expect them to start from their arrested motion and continue the dance. They seem to be carried away by the music, the dance, and each other – transported into the seclusion of a lavender mist. Yet they are transformed into decorative abstractions which recall the effect of the colourful patterns of the light show falling upon the crowds in the dance hall. This engaging picture is set not in a border but is held in a space by the delicate grip of the sinuous lettering. And the dancers are part of this space, with their feet on the "ground" and their heads in the stars. For its relevant theme, its imaginative concept, and its thorough execution, this *tour de force* of graphic abstraction ranks among the most outstanding works of the rock poster art.

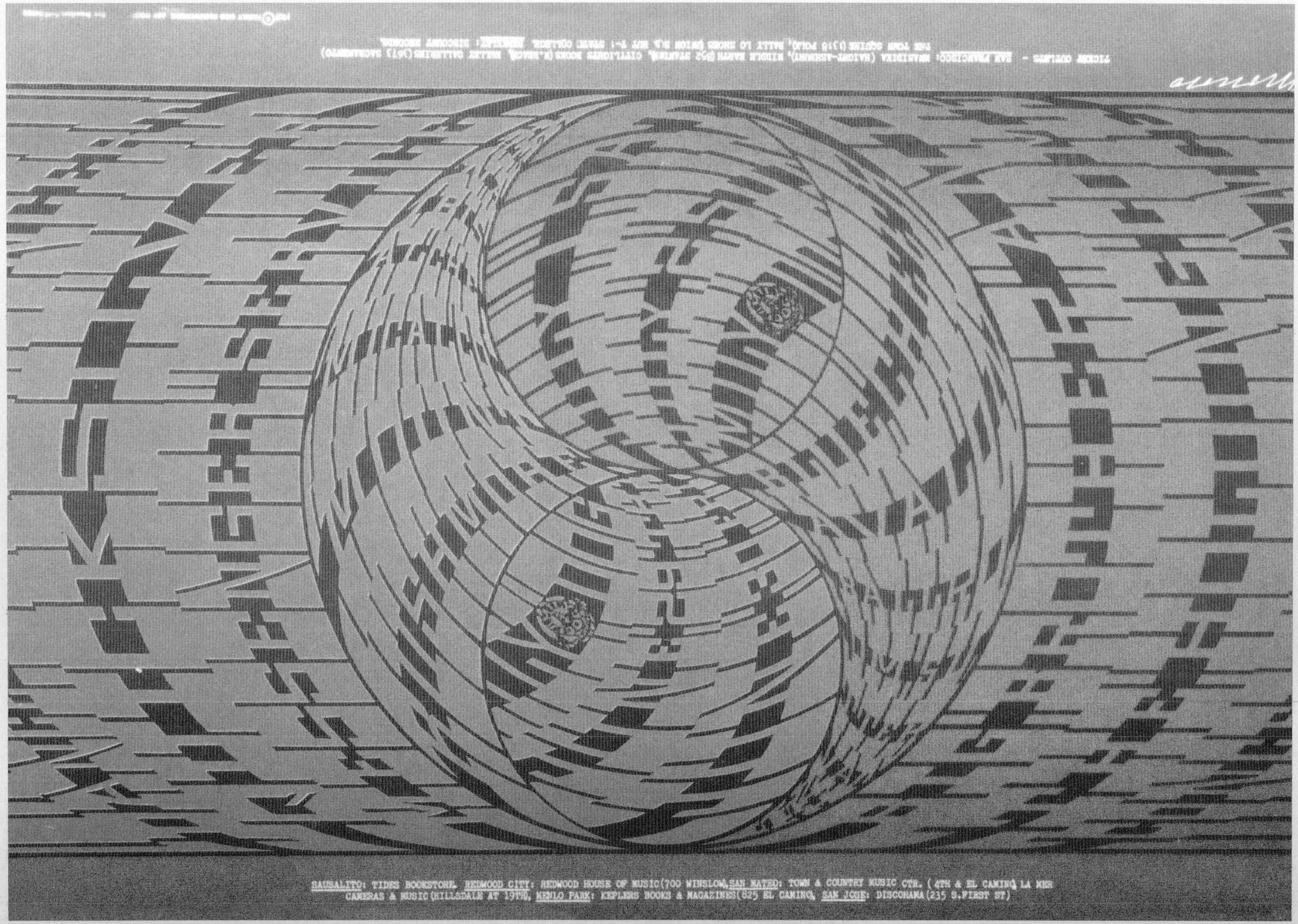

SAUSALITO: TIDES BOOKSTORE. REDWOOD CITY: REDWOOD HOUSE OF MUSIC(700 WINSLOW),SAN MATEO: TOWN & COUNTRY MUSIC CTR. (4TH & EL CAMINO) LA MER
CAMERAS & MUSIC(HILLSDALE AT 19TH), MENLO PARK: KEPLERS BOOKS & MAGAZINES(825 EL CAMINO), SAN JOSE: DISCOHAMA(235 S.FIRST ST)

↻ 'The Doors', the Matrix, Victor Moscoso, Neon Rose Series – 1967

↻ 'Neptunes Notion', Moby Grape, Charlatans, Avalon Ballroom, Victor Moscoso – 1967 FD 49

↻ 'Mist Dance', Youngbloods, Avalon Ballroom, Victor Moscoso – 1967 FD 81

Moscoso retained the use of Wilson-type lettering, even in later works when it was appropriate to the form, but by his second month of production he began to settle on a lettering style of his own. It was basically a simple upper case letter to which Moscoso applied large, sometimes massive serifs. This basic form afforded him considerable flexibility and he used it effectively in a variety of ways, as a dense rectilinear block, or stretched into freeform and curvilinear shapes. The massive serifs and hot colour sometimes made the lettering disappear into the background. In his later posters he often shaped the lettering into the form of a leaf or flower petal. The flower is a very relevant image for these hippie posters but it is a measure of the artists' creativity that it was never used as a trivial or sentimental symbol. In Moscoso's use of it, any symbolic value it may contain is only a minimal, background aspect – it is always dominated by a design idea, which emphasises it as a thing in itself, or as a decorative abstraction.

Moscoso exploited the techniques of modern lithography more than any other artist. He explored complex colour effects, such as building up an image through "overprinting", and through a series of developments this brought an unexpected dimension to the poster art. Due to the colour overprinting technique, images had the sensational effect of turning off and on when seen in the flashing coloured lights of the dance hall, and one of these created an illusion of movement. Moscoso's development of this animation technique in several later designs further transformed the rock poster from a static, independent art form into an active, visual element of the dance environment, an extension of the light show. In addition to the individual artistic achievement and the creative sponsorship of the client, these posters can be appreciated as a brilliant expression of the unique intensity, the high physical and psychic energy which characterised the San Francisco rock scene, and which came together in the dance halls. © *Walter Medeiros 1976*

RICK GRIFFIN

by Walter Medeiros

Rick Griffin was aware of the gathering energy in San Francisco. He had passed through the Red Dog Saloon scene and then returned to Southern California, where he had grown up in the surfing culture and later worked as a staff artist for *Surfer* magazine. By mid 1966 the San Francisco rock posters began to hit southern California. Griffin was impressed, especially by the art of Mouse Studios, and he decided to come to San Francisco and participate in the graphic renaissance. Shortly after he arrived, he produced a poster for the "Human Be-In", the first large counterculture gathering. Griffin was already familiar with the new tribal consciousness.

For the past year or so he had been living with an earthy tribe called the Jook Savages, some of whom were very serious in their identification with Indians. With this background and the tribal theme of the event, it was natural that Griffin's "Be-In" poster should develop the Indian motif. Griffin's first poster for the Psychedelic Shop is a graphic compendium of hippie culture and his own background and style. In addition to the Indian frontier elements, it contains various psychedelic and metaphysical references, hippie emblems, and a bit of that special mode of psychedelic wit (and a favourite mode of Griffin's) – the pun.

These early works demonstrate that Griffin was already an excellent draftsman and an imaginative designer. His formal training was minimal: his graphic skill is apparently a matter of natural aptitude and parental support. His father, an engineer, was also a skilled artist and an amateur archaeologist; the family took frequent trips to the Southwest, visiting ghost towns and obscure archaeological sites. From this experience Griffin absorbed the lore, the forms, and the feeling of the cultures of the American West – both that of the native Americans and the nineteenth century settlers.

🎧 'Heart And Torch', Big Brother And The Holding Company, Fillmore West, Rick Griffin – 1968 BG 136

☾ 'Aoxomoxoa', Grateful Dead, Soundproof Productions, Avalon Ballroom. Printer's proof with handbills, Rick Griffin – 1969

☾☾ Rick Griffin
PHOTO: GENE ANTHONY

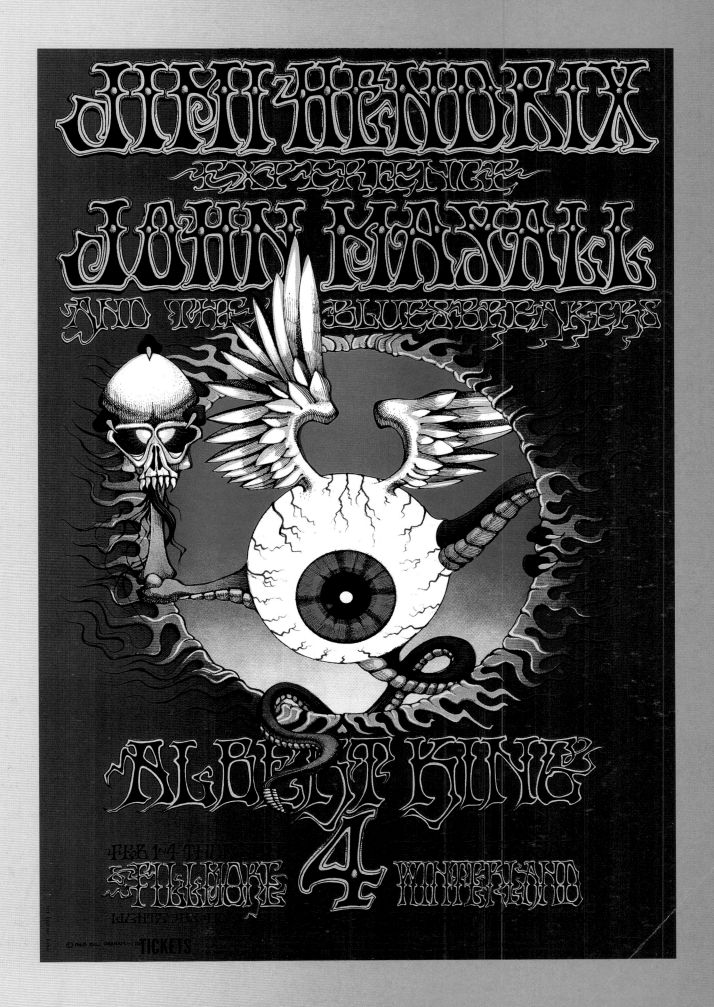

🎧 'Flying Eyeball', Jimi Hendrix Experience, Fillmore Auditorium and Winterland, Fillmore West, Rick Griffin – 1968 BG 105

➲➲ Jimi Hendrix
Experience, Winterland,
Rick Griffin and
Victor Moscoso
– 1968 BG 140

➲ 'Morning Paper',
Quicksilver Messenger
Service, Avalon
Ballroom, Rick Griffin
– 1967 FD 89

➲ Moody Blues,
Fillmore West, Rick
Griffin and Alton Kelley
– 1968 BG 146

Two months after the "Be-In" Griffin began designing for the Family Dog. In most of his early posters he used the familiar nineteenth century lettering and formats, as in the 'Gold-rush' and 'Sutters Mill' designs. These are also dope puns: the "rush" of 'Acapulco Gold' and the floating "pot", and in the latter design the old-timer is not panning for gold but straining the seeds of "gold" from his sack. At this time Griffin also produced several "dope ad" posters, which contain puns and fine still life drawings of smoking accoutrements.

Griffin also took up the advertising style, usually in collaboration with George Hunter of The Charlatans. The 'Sparrow Canned Heat' poster is a combination of Hunter's ideas and Griffin's artwork, as is the unusual "triptych" design. Griffin's old tribe, the Jook Savages, moved up north, too, and when their funky, improvisational "Jug band" made an appearance in connection with The Charlatans, Griffin produced a more light-hearted commercial pun, and some delightful caricatures of the groups.

Another source of Griffin's art is commonplace imagery and symbols, ranging from Mickey Mouse to the metaphysical.

Griffin was fond of certain product labels, primarily kitchen products, for reasons of their friendly, unpretentious images and the care with which they were drawn. It was as though the trademark images of these domestic staples were broadly symbolic of care, beginning with care about one's work and extending to family love and human brotherhood. These trademark figures and many others, including some by his poster "art brothers", were celebrated in a compendium of his favourite images over which he inscribed: "Everybody is good at heart."

Griffin first combined a variety of commonplace images in the 'Independence' poster, which was inspired by a Fourth of July dance. Griffin wasn't a flag-waver of course, but like the more thoughtful hippies, he had a great respect for this land, its people, and its revolutionary, political-spiritual principles. The patriotic holiday provided the opportunity to get high on various relevant ideas and images, and he produced a powerful heraldic emblem that is an impressive display of skill in design and drawing.

In a later poster Griffin exploited popular imagery of a lighter sort. Based on the front page of the local Sunday's comic section he created a mind-blowing sequence of panels which have, at most, only minimal visual links and characters which speak in an abstract, nonsensical script. The graphic play and the visual/mental impact of the nonsense lettering was exploited further in subsequent posters. It is a collaborative design that is the height of psychedelic abstraction. This minimally functional poster ranks

↻↻ 'Pow Wow',
Human Be-in,
Golden Gate Park, SF,
Rick Griffin – 1967

↻ 'Aunt Jemima',
Big Brother And The
Holding Company,
Rick Griffin – 1967 FD 65

↻ 'Three Indian
Dudes', Grateful Dead,
Avalon Ballroom,
Rick Griffin – 1967 FD 54

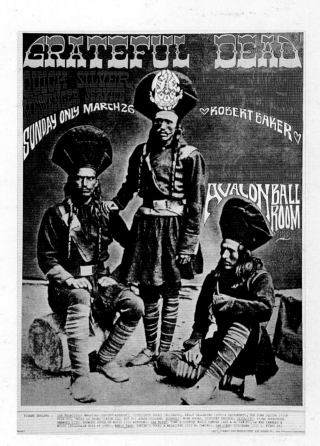

with Wilson's 'Golden Lady' as an example of the music pro-moters' acceptance of art as a primary value.

As Griffin matured in the handling of commonplace imagery he began to assemble strong images into strange and sometimes ominous designs which appear as abstract, personally expressive symbols. These designs are usually focused around a central point or axis – which enhances their visual impact, and the forms are powerfully rendered as very concrete, three-dimensional objects. The simple 'Heart And Torch' is a strange but beautifully radiant design which seems to affirm that knowledge and goodness come from within.

A couple of Griffin's creations come right out at you, such as the weird and funky monster who offers a pill with "pay attention" printed on it. Shortly afterward he produced a heavier version of this format in which a winged eyeball with a rattler's tail emerges from a flaming hole holding a skull. This design marks a dramatic change in the feeling of Griffin's art. During the following year of intermittent production he created some light-hearted designs, but several of these later works are powerful, bizarre assemblages that appear to express an intense concern with the awesome realities of life, such as its very existence, its scheme of mortality, and its continuity. In one such design the eyeball, skull and snake were combined in a frightful, static, totem-like figure that appears as a triumph of death. There is a level of interpretation at which the honour of these symbols can be dispelled, but even so, the image remains grave, like a vision of Kali.

Among Griffin's last San Francisco posters is one for The Grateful Dead, whose name doubtless added inspiration to the artist's development of a familiar theme. Here again Griffin's vivid imagination and graphic skill combined to create a design that strikes with the clarity of a vision. Death flashes its knowing smile, but the white-hot sun competes for our attention. Death claims its eggs – the beginning contains the end – but not before a seed is loosed. And Death's body is aum, the beetle/scarab works below, and on either side the earth is rich with life-plump forms. It's like a cross-section through the cosmic plan. The design is balanced with classic order and the cycle goes on endlessly under the blazing eye of light. © *Walter Medeiros 1976*

RANDY TUTEN

by Walter Medeiros

↻ 'Sutter's Mill', Quicksilver
Messenger Service, Avalon Ballroom,
Rick Griffin – 1967 FD 62

⤵ 'Hell's Angels Annual Party',
Longshoreman's Hall, San Francisco,
Randy Tuten – 1971

↻ Steve Miller Band tour poster,
Randy Tuten – 1991 BGP

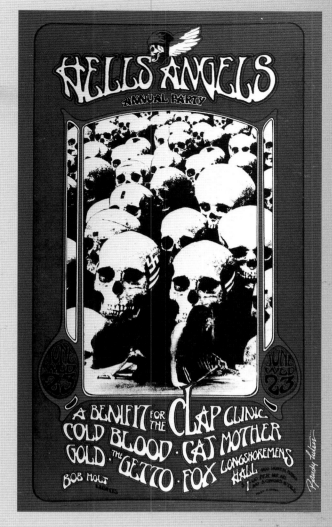

The latter two and a half years of Fillmore West productions provided the opportunity for three more artists to develop. The first of these was Randy Tuten, who began production in early 1969. Tuten was a Los Angeles "street kid" and a self-taught artist who, like Rick Griffin, was attracted to San Francisco by the poster art, primarily that of Mouse Studios. Although Tuten's posters show considerable variety, his formats and lettering style generally reflect the influence of early twentieth century product labels and the related styles of Mouse, and sometimes Griffin. Tuten's own taste, sense of proportion, and craftsmanship imparted new vigour to these conventional classical forms and produced a distinctive personal style. Essentially, his art is an extension of fine old commercial art and his posters often attain a strength and originality comparable to that of the earlier rock poster artists who worked in this style.

A few of Tuten's posters revived the advertising style directly, and many others are developments of typical label formats. The 'Medicine Kid' design is perhaps the best of this type, for both its wit and its art, especially the large lettering. This conventional, but distinctive lettering, recalls those early days of this century when countless commercial artists sat at their boards applying their invention to the rather limited range of lettering styles which were then acceptable, trying to devise something unique, some "flair" in order to attain distinction for the product and themselves. Although Tuten often exploited such standard lettering he also developed a unique style, which ranges from the robust and funky to the flowing and delicate.

Orderliness and clarity are typical of Tuten's art, but he didn't restrict himself to the old-time commercial style. His originality and diverse approach are apparent from his earliest works, some of which contain strange, collaged environments, such as the Queen Mary framed in a doorway. There is no heavy personal meaning in Tuten's art, but he often includes strong images of things he likes, and chief among these are large, powerful and fine transportation devices. He is a realist, too, and doesn't shun

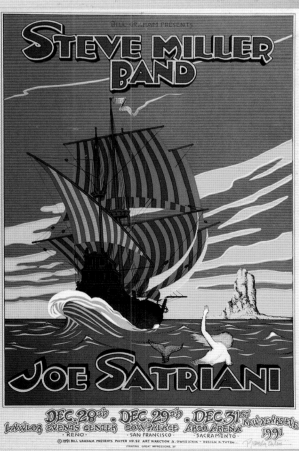

↷↷ Grateful Dead,
Fillmore West,
Randy Tuten – 1969
BG 154

↷ Jeff Beck Group,
Fillmore West, Randy
Tuten – 1969 BG 168

↻ Led Zeppelin,
Bonzo Dog Band,
Winterland and Oakland
Coliseum, Randy
Tuten – 1969 BG 199

the fascination and visual impact of the disasters, which occur to these prideful objects, such as great ships.

The image-power of such an event is exploited in the 'Titanic' design. In collaboration with artist D Bread, the form of the classic 1948 Lincoln automobile was featured in an Art Deco context, and a 1940s jukebox inspired a Deco border. As the original poster artists had revived Victorian graphics, these "second wave" artists were the first to revive the decorative style of the Streamline era.

Tuten's posters often related to the bands or the event, either through a performer's photo or associated imagery. For a Grateful Dead benefit and a Hell's Angels party he produced a variation on the skull image which symbolised each of those groups. He put the rock 'n' roll "gang", Sha-na-na, behind bars, and for a Country Joe And The Fish concert he created a classic design which expresses the strong political orientation of this Berkeley band and also depicts the police action which was then common in that city.

Such heavy or serious images comprise only a small portion of Tuten's work. A more personally expressive side of him is reflected in several posters which contain funky, off-the-wall humour, such as the image of the hamburger, the avocado with "googly" eyes, and the monstrous wrestlers holding the delicate ladies. Women otherwise fared much better in his art, however in one design he used the charming photo of a friend, and in another, a picture of a lady he would have liked to have met. Both of these are presented in unique, classical formats, and in his only poster which contains Indians, he demonstrated his ability to also treat this traditional theme with freshness and dignity. Simple as they are, these modest handbills rank among Tuten's best works. The strong design and appropriate lettering styles greatly enhance the antique photos, transforming these common subjects into new and deeply satisfying works of graphic art. © *Walter Medeiros 1976*

From 1976, when Medeiros wrote the San Francisco MOMA exhibit catalogue, to the present, Tuten has continued to be among the most prolific of San Francisco poster artists. He has drawn many memorable posters for major performers who have appeared at venues promoted by the Bill Graham organisation. He has also been commissioned to create posters for other groups, as well as commemorative artworks for musical groups who would only approve his efforts to visually celebrate their accomplishments. Many of the younger poster artists who have achieved some success and prominence over the past ten years hold Tuten's work in awe. The general consensus in the rock art community is that he has continued to grow as an artist and may be doing his best, most creative and exciting work at the present time.

GARY GRIMSHAW

Born in Detroit in 1944, Grimshaw was the primary poster and light show artist for Detroit's legendary Grande Ballroom through 1969, and like Tuten continues his prolific and brilliant work up to the present. Gary was also heavily and personally involved in the political struggles of the late Sixties and Seventies, and deep commitment to the causes of peace and social justice have also been maintained over the years.

After graduating from high school and spending a year working in a steel mill, Gary enlisted in the US Navy. He was stationed aboard the aircraft carrier *Coral Sea* during the Vietnam War (1964-1966), and spent seven months in the war zone. He passed the last portion of his service in San Francisco, where his ship had returned to dry-dock for repairs. He explained how he immediately became caught up in the newly emerging Bay Area political/cultural scene:

"The first day I had liberty, the headlines in the Hearst papers were 'Peace March Today', because it was the day of the second big Berkeley Peace March from the campus to Oakland. The first one had ended in a riot where the Hell's Angels were beating up the peaceniks while the Oakland Police just stood around watching. After that, Allen Ginsberg went over to the Hell's Angels and got them to participate in the next one. I got some civilian clothes, took a bus over to Berkeley, and just marched with the march. It was the first day I was back and it was fascinating. I was aware of the Beat culture in the Fifties, and I was aware of what the left/hip culture was like, but I'd never seen anything on such a mass scale. There were probably five or six thousand people in the march and the whole circus surrounding it. I went to Detroit several times from 1966-1970, but most of that time I lived in the Bay Area."

🎧 Gary Grimshaw pictured in 1996

➲ 'Mod Man', MC5, Grande Ballroom, Detroit, Gary Grimshaw – 1966

➲➲ 'Sun Ra', MC5, Wayne State University, Gary Grimshaw – 1967

During this early spell in San Francisco, Grimshaw attended shows at the Fillmore and Avalon venues, and quickly became aware of the emerging psychedelic poster scene as new examples appeared daily on buses, telephone poles and in store windows. Gary's art awareness had begun at an early age, when as a student he learned "on the job" working at his uncle's printing shop in Dearborn, Michigan. (In later years it printed all of the Grande Ballroom series of posters.) Other family members were involved with graphic art and design. In high school he produced T-shirts with his close friend Rob Tyner, lead singer for the famous and brilliant MC5. He explained: "We didn't have airbrushes so we'd draw them with permanent markers. He would draw them and I would fill them in…It wasn't a business, though. The first art job that I actually got paid for was the first Grande Ballroom poster, for the first Grande Ballroom show, which was The MC5 in 1966."

SUN RA

AND HIS MYTH SCIENCE ARKESTRA

IN CONCERT WITH THE

MC5

SUNDAY JUNE 18
COMMUNITY ARTS AUD. W.S.U. 8:00
LIGHTS BY THE MAGIC VEIL - ADM. 2.00
PRESENTED BY TRANS-LOVE SPONSOR - WSU ARTISTS' SOCIETY

Gary Grimshaw

POSTER BY GRIMSHAW

During his post-Navy sojourn in San Francisco, Grimshaw was the art director for thirteen issues of the famous underground newspaper *The San Francisco Oracle*, and also did work for the politically engaged weekly, *The Berkeley Tribe*. After his return to Detroit, Gary initially became involved with the Grande Ballroom by doing the light show every weekend.

well as they could've been. I think I started out at about $25 for a poster design, and by '69 I eventually got up to about $75. The average payment for artwork was $35 or $40. At that time the Avalon and Fillmore were paying between $200 and $300. The Grande budget was minuscule compared to that. Also, the Avalon and Fillmore would book far enough ahead that they could

⌾ Mind-Zap, Grande Ballroom, Gary Grimshaw – 1966

⌾ Detroit Rock 'N' Roll Revival, Gary Grimshaw – 1997

⌾⌾ Grateful Dead, University of Michigan, Gary Grimshaw – 1971

However he also soon became involved in creating the posters for the Grande shows. Gary explained:

"Russ Gibb depended pretty much on the posters. But he had a network of high school students to help with distribution. He built this up so that when the cards came out they would just be distributed in a pyramid system and they'd go through all the high schools in Detroit. The students were pretty organised. They'd get a stack of cards, pass them out in school and then they'd get into the Grande free.

"They started out doing both [posters and handbills]. But since posters are good in storefronts and since Plum Street was probably the only place where there was foot traffic, the posters weren't really functional. They did maybe a dozen posters and cards before they switched to cards only.

"The Grande stuff was all done in one day – tops. As soon as I got the information I just started working on it and didn't stop until it was done. I'd take it to the printer and come home and crash. It was just panic, I didn't even have time to think about it, which is probably good because the first impulse about a design is usually right. It's just that they weren't executed as

give the artists two or three weeks to work on the posters. So these were done under a lot more difficult circumstances."

During the late Sixties Grimshaw also created art for Detroit's notorious rock 'n' roll band The MC5. Simultaneously, Gary continued his connection with the San Francisco Bay Area with frequent trips out west. Inspiration from the Civil Rights movement and the struggle of Native Americans led to his engagement with the White Panther Party (WPP) in the role of Minister of Art. Daily he worked to create the national newspaper of the Party, *Sun/Dance*, and *The Sun* weekly.

WPP chairman John Sinclair in Michigan had been convicted and sentenced to ten years imprisonment for possession of two joints of marijuana. Freeing John became a full time effort, and Gary joined with a broad-based coalition that resulted in The John Sinclair Freedom Rally. The performers included John Lennon and Yoko Ono, Stevie Wonder, Bob Seger and many others in December 1971. Within days, the Michigan State Legislature reduced the penalties for possession from a felony to a misdemeanour and John was free.

Subsequently Grimshaw became the art director for the Ann Arbor Blues and Jazz Festivals in 1972 and 1973. Working with the Rainbow People's Party and Rainbow Productions (evolutions of the White Panthers) he created graphics for

concerts, bands, community organisations, clubs and publications throughout the Mid West from his headquarters in Ann Arbor. In 1974 Gary returned to his hometown Detroit and concentrated on the thriving rock 'n' roll scene. For the next fourteen years he produced posters, recording packages, logos and graphics for all of the major promoters and dozens of bands and clubs in the Motor City. Gary was also associate art director for *Creem* magazine from 1976 to 1984.

Always interested in new music, the emerging punk/alternative music scene in Detroit was a special thrill to Gary. He became the flyer artist for Bookies Club 870 and Traxx, two main venues for this music in the early days. This led to a long-term association with Ceremony Productions, who continue to be Detroit's premier alternative rock promoters at multiple venues.

In 1984 Grimshaw, along with John Sinclair and Frank Bach, formed MSA (Music/Media Services Associates), a full service agency that had among its clients The City Of Detroit Summer Festivals, Chene Park Riverfront Concert Series, The Music Hall Theatre, and several bands and clubs. The agency also held special event productions such as the Detroit For Africa concert.

In 1989 and Gary and his wife Laura relocated to San Francisco. Since returning to the Bay Area, Grimshaw has continued freelancing, and has created new and exciting artworks. He embarked on a programme of reprinting his early concert posters, and has since self-published thirty-four new and reprinted posters, issued a mail-order catalogue, and created four new poster designs for Bill Graham Presents concerts. He has also done CD cover art for A&M, River Road, Alive/Total Energy and Bopological Records as well as logo and T-shirt work for several music artists and Polydor.

Exhibitions of Gary's work include three one-man shows in Detroit in 1984, 1987 and 1996. Group exhibitions include: The Detroit Institute Of Arts in 1974 and 1980; The Motor City Joint Show with Stanley Mouse, Wes Wilson and Mark Arminski in 1993; The San Francisco Rock Poster Expo in 1992, 1993 and 1994; The Temporary Insanity Show in San Francisco in 1995; and The Visual Jams Show during the opening of The Rock 'N' Roll Hall Of Fame and museum in Cleveland in 1995. His work is part of the permanent display in the museum.

Most recently, Gary has been art-directing promotional materials for the upcoming full-length film *MC5: A True Testimonial* being produced by Future/Now Films. He is working on a new catalogue, CD covers, new poster commissions and more poster reprints and can be visited on the internet at earthlink.net – all in the name of commercial art. "The work I do is mass art, as opposed to fine art," he explained. It isn't for display in a gallery, it's for printing. Commercial art is a good medium for what's going on, and it's more democratic than fine art because it isn't exclusive. There are thousands of copies of each work, so anyone can see or even own it. When I do a poster, there's input from the promoter, the band, a lot of people other than me. I am a team player, but I can pick which team I want to be on."

◐ Eric Burdon and
The Animals,
Grande Ballroom,
Gary Grimshaw – 1968

◑ Paupers, MC5,
Grande Ballroom,
Gary Grimshaw – 1967

DAVID SINGER

by Walter Medeiros

➲ Miles Davis,
Fillmore West,
David Singer – 1971
BG 279

➲➲ Humble Pie,
Fillmore West,
David Singer – 1971
BG 280

During the last two years of the Fillmore, most of the posters were produced by David Singer, a rather quiet young man who had grown up in Quakertown, Pennsylvania. During his high school years he was part of the local street culture, and later he joined the Navy for a change of scene. His last duty station was San Francisco and he settled here in 1964. He had some experience in graphic art, but didn't consider himself an artist. The high energy and creativity of the hippie scene gave him inspiration and self-confidence and he began making collages with images cut from magazines. In early 1969 he took his portfolio to show Bill Graham, which resulted in an immediate commission for a series of a dozen posters.

These posters appear to be a world apart from the rock 'n' roll scene and the traditions of the poster art; dense pattern, intense colour, decorative lettering and funky humour are all absent. Singer's pictorial style displays a new form of classical order and restraint. The imagery and colour tone are cool and reserved and the visual impact of these posters is much less immediate. What they lack in surface intensity is balanced by depth, however, from the first quiet appreciation of the whole collage to the reflective process which the imagery induces.

The style and content of Singer's collages are consistent throughout his work but the lettering shows an interesting development. Unfamiliar with lettering at first, he chose the slim, geometrical letter style from Tuten and Bread's '48 Lincoln' poster and used it in a standardised format. Later he developed other slender shapes, including free-hand curvilinear styles, and eventually he began to relate the lettering to the imagery. Among his last works are several in which drawing and flowing decoration are predominant. In the 'Closing Week' poster the major lettering is exceptionally decorative and original, yet it has a certain familiarity, like the hand of Stanley Mouse.

BILL GRAHAM PRESENTS IN SAN FRANCISCO

HUMBLE PIE
SWAMP DOGG
SHANTI

LIGHTS BY PRISMATIC REVENGE

MAY 13·14·15·16 FILLMORE WEST

© BILL GRAHAM 1971 · #280   TICKETS   TEA LAUTREC LITHO · SAN FRANCISCO
ALL MACY'S TICKET OUTLETS · · SAN FRANCISCO · FOX PLAZA BOX OFFICE NINTH & MARKET · CITY LIGHTS BOOKSTORE 261 COLUMBUS AVE · THE TOWN SQUIRE
1318 POLK · OUTSIDE IN 2544 MISSION   BERKELEY · DISCOUNT RECORDS · SHAKESPEARE & CO   SAUSALITO · THE TIDES   REDWOOD CITY · REDWOOD HOUSE
OF MUSIC   SAN MATEO · TOWN & COUNTRY RECORDS   SAN JOSE · DISCOUNT RECORDS   MENLO PARK · DISCOUNT RECORDS   SAN RAFAEL · RECORD KING
NEW OUTLETS: SAN FRANCISCO · MUSIC ODYSSEY 3628 GEARY   SINGER   OAKLAND · SHERMAN CLAY   HAYWARD · GENERAL STORE 24518 MISSION

↻ BB King, Santana,
Fillmore West,
David Singer – 1969
BG 181

↻ Johnny Winter,
Fillmore West,
David Singer – 1969
BG 180

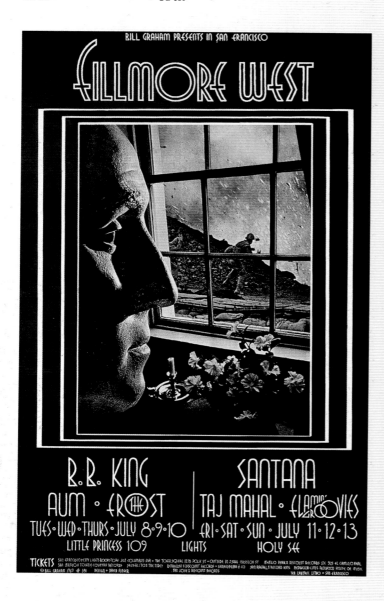

There is wide variety in Singer's collages, and although some can be related to the bands or to an event, most of them are independent works of art, simple play with fern or favourite images. The 'Tulips' design is about voluptuous beauty and a word pun, but it is a visual statement, not a literal one. Singer is fond of animals, especially birds and cats, and these appear in several posters. There is a quietly bizarre domestic scene with a monstrous house cat, and in the poster with the soft blue frame a white horse frolics in some wild Eden behind an ancient monument to its being. Animals are featured in Bill Graham's 'Closing Week' poster in the enigmatic collage, and also in the decorative birds, which derive from Singer's awareness of Pennsylvanian Dutch folk art.

Singer's collages are not direct products of psychedelic experience, but they partake of that consciousness. The collages are open and involving and, despite their variety, may evoke a serious, reflective mood. The human figure appears everywhere: a child in a verdant field, a maid of summer whose play and reflection seem to evoke an awareness of her body's season, an astronaut plodding through some alternative reality. Certain other images are prominent: the sky; the sun or moon; a galaxy; the sea; deserts and plains; ancient ruins and classical art; a shadow of human form. Vastness, stillness, the eternal and the transitory; theme impressions resonate deep within the psyche, evoking that awe of the cosmic reality-mystery which brings us to meditative silence.

This mood is the exact opposite of that which the original poster art projected. By 1969 the energetic outsiders who had brought the scene together had mostly moved on to other frontiers. During the last few years the Fillmore audiences were largely composed of high school and college youth, and Singer's style

☻ Chambers Brothers,
Fillmore West,
David Singer – 1969
BG 206

☻ Chicago, Fillmore
West and Winterland,
David Singer – 1970
BG 225

☻☻ Chuck Berry,
Fillmore West,
David Singer – 1970
BG 250

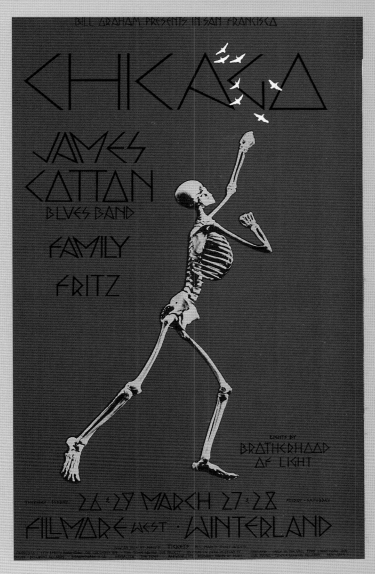

can be seen as an artistic parallel to the popularisation of rock music and other hippie values. With Singer's posters the art-form changed from a style uniquely expressive of a small, intensely active underground culture to a form closer to "fine art" consciousness. Superficially, this might appear as a decline from the high style of rock poster art but it can also be seen as a natural and positive development, since Singer's art is more accessible to a general audience.

Changes came down everywhere. In 1969, Bob Dylan, that old restless rebel, was crooning, "Tonight I'll be staying here with you." Expansion, diversity, and energy was what this youth movement was about. The scene expanded, the energy changed and variety happened all by itself. And David Singer was part of that outward, and inward, movement. © *Walter Medeiros 1976*

MICHAEL BOWEN

➲ 'Yantra! India',
hand painted etching,
Michael Bowen – 1975

➲ Michael Bowen in
front of 'Wizard' – 1966
PHOTO: GENE ANTHONY

Michael Bowen was without doubt one of an elite core of art innovators on the San Francisco scene. His home was regularly visited by the likes of Ginsberg, Leary, Alpert and Allen Cohen. Cohen published the San Francisco underground paper *The Oracle* which operated out of Bowen's SF home. Bowen contributed much of the art for *The Oracle*'s colourful pages. Michael Bowen conceived the Human Be In Festival hosting the event featuring his friends Ginsberg, Gary Snyder and Tim Leary. It was for this event that he created 'The Human Be-In' poster with Stanley Mouse and Casey Sonnabend.

Michael Bowen's work as an artist spans several decades and has been progressively documented in exhibitions, reviews, art periodicals and in the media. He has exhibited in the United States and abroad, has a large following, and his work is housed by groups of private collectors and museums. He is considered one of the foremost core catalysts in avant-garde art circles throughout the world. He was a youthful member of the abstract/assemblage group in the early Fifties in Los Angeles, travelled to the east coast and Europe in the early Sixties, and completed four world art tours between 1969 and 1988. Travelling to Japan, Cambodia and India, he acted as a liaison in bringing together a fusion of eastern and western visual symbology. His etching series has been compared to Chagall, Fuchs, Fini and Dali; works which comprise over ninety-five different editions in full colour. In the mid Seventies, he turned his attention to the world of psychic phenomenon and allied himself with the PSI Art Group, Ingo Swan, Hechelmann and Schwertberger. The sensitivity of Michael Bowen's work provided direction and inspiration to the poets and writers of the mid Fifties such as

Allen Ginsberg, Michael McClure and Gary Snyder. His involvement with this movement has been chronicled in a wide spectrum of literary/art publications and established Michael Bowen as an artistic cultural hero. Bowen is currently utilising new skills such as air brush technique to widen the spectrum of his abilities. He resides in San Francisco, California and the island of Hawaii, in the Hawaiian chain.

Exhibitions include: Beat Culture In The New America, 1950-65, Whitney Museum of American Art, New York; Fine Art Museum of San Francisco; Walker Art Centre, Minneapolis. Artists exhibited with Michael Bowen include: Jackson Pollock, Edward Keinhole, Francs Kline, Wallace Berman, Dennis Hopper, Jim Dine, Jack Kerouac, William Burroughs, Brian Gysin and Arthur Monroe.

⊙ 'Pele, Goddess Of The Volcano', Hawaii, oil on canvas, Michael Bowen – 1984

⊃ 'Master Of The Masks', Nepalese Experience, etching, Michael Bowen – 1974

⊃⊃ 'Moon', Big Island Hawaii, oil on canvas, Michael Bowen – 1970

⌒ 'Kali, India', oil on canvas, Michael Bowen – 1983

THE AMERICAN SCENE : MICHAEL BOWEN

BOB SCHNEPF

by Walter Medeiros

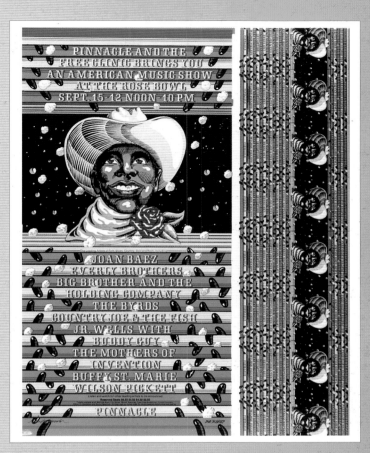

Bob Schnepf was the third member of what might be called "the professionals" among the poster artists. He had also studied at Cooper Union and had come to the San Francisco Art Institute in 1961 to complete his training as a painter. In 1965, after travelling back and forth to New York, and later to Europe, he settled in a rural district of the Bay Area. There a process of change, which had been occurring during these years, came to a conclusion. The relaxed attitude and lifestyle of California, his psychedelic experiences, and his realisation of the absurdity of the picture-making and art gallery game eventually caused him to change from painting in an abstract expressionist style to drawing and painting images once again. He began producing psychedelic postcards for head shops and simple posters for local rock music clubs. During his occasional visits to San Francisco he met the other poster artists. He was encouraged by their support, especially by Moscoso's technical advice, and eventually he obtained commissions from the Family Dog.

With his first design he emerged as a mature poster artist, able to present original ideas and develop traditional forms. The lettering in his first poster is derived from Wilson's, but it has been transformed into a crisp, elegant style, which marks it as the work of a

distinctive hand. The colour scheme is familiar too, but this element has also been handled with sufficient mastery to establish it as a unique and independent work. The image is entirely his own. It's a psychedelic vision, specifically relevant to the dance, and generally expressive of the joyous exuberance, which Schnepf experienced during the early, high years of the hippie culture.

In most of Schnepf's posters the imagery usually relates to the culture in general rather than to the specific event. Occasionally he did produce a design based on the groups, such as 'The Dancing Bear'. The event for which this was intended had a band of that name on the bill, but that job fell through and the design was used for a "quickie" poster for the Family Dog. Schnepf's professional draftsmanship is apparent in the background drawing and in the precision of the handsome, slender lettering. On his next poster the band names (and their

🔗 Pinnacle concert poster, original artwork for poster and handbills, Bob Schnepf and John van Hamersveld – 1968

music) gave him a strong visual impression, including colour, and he skilfully combined the imagery, lettering, and colour into a subtle, sensuously beautiful design. It is the finest poster of its type.

Two months later Schnepf designed his seventh and last Family Dog poster, shortly after they had returned to production of black and white posters only. Colour was important to Schnepf and affected by this decline in the Family Dog's fortunes, he didn't actively pursue other poster work. He had approached the Fillmore and was well received, but no commissions resulted. Of all the major artists Schnepf produced the least. He did produce about half a dozen additional posters for miscellaneous promoters and also several record album covers, but it is unfortunate that such an excellent designer disappeared from the poster movement so soon. © *Walter Medeiros 1976*

BONNIE MACLEAN

by Walter Medeiros

↻ Pink Floyd, Fillmore Auditorium, Bonnie MacLean – 1967 BG 90

☯ Big Brother And The Holding Company, Fillmore, Bonnie MacLean – 1967 BG 65

↻ Muddy Waters, Fillmore Auditorium, Bonnie MacLean – 1967 BG 76

➲ Eric Burdon, Fillmore, Bonnie MacLean – 1967 BG 89

After Wilson quit the Fillmore in May of 1967, most of the posters for the remainder of that year were designed by Bonnie MacLean, a Fillmore staff member. The thirty posters she produced established her as the only woman artist of note. With few exceptions, her designs were largely derived from Wilson's art. She was sufficiently skilled for a novice poster designer, but her work does not appear to have been based in a strong artistic identity. Her unique contribution to poster art was the introduction of Medieval, Gothic and antique forms.

MacLean produced some interesting posters in Wilson's style and in her early designs she often combined the two elements. Gothic architectural decoration dominated her first poster, and in her second design she set three merging female heads and a rounded body of lettering upon a flat background of traditional decorative forms. The priest or priestess image often occurs in her work and in her third and most elegant poster she created a very sensitive and exotic figure. In a later design, which appears to include a "door" motif, she achieved some expressive faces in Wilson's printerly drawing style.

With her seventh poster she achieved her most striking design. Everything is essentially Wilson-derived, but here the forms have been sufficiently simplified and transformed to attain an identity and power of their own. The composition, colour, and the dynamic "worm's eye" view are all well handled and the powerful presence of the massive, looming figures evokes the immediacy of an LSD vision. Near the end of her career she produced another exceptional work, and one of complete originality. The straightforward lettering is refreshing and effective, as is the whole design. The face projects a strong character and has pleasing colour, especially in contrast to the black background. This type of collage-like composition was common among hippie artists but this is the first such example to appear in the posters. In retrospect, it can be seen as an illustrator's version of Wilson's merging-figures motif and as a precursor of the bizarre assemblages of Lee Conklin. © *Walter Medeiros 1976*

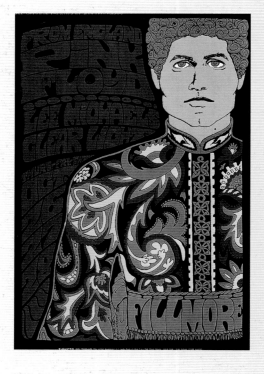

ERIC BURDON AND THE MOTHERS YOUR BIRTHDAY FLASH

THURS-FRI-SAT OCT 19-20-21 LIGHTS BY HOLY SEE FILLMORE

B. MACLEAN © BILL GRAHAM 1967 #89

TICKETS SAN FRANCISCO: City Lights Bookstore; S.F. State College (Hut T-1); The Town Squre 1318 Polk; Wild Colors (1418 Haight); Bally Lo (Union Square); HAYWARD: Matsuri; BERKELEY: Discount Records; Shakespeare & Co.; SAN MATEO: Town & County Records; REDWOOD CITY: Redwood House of Music; PALO ALTO: Dana Morgan Music; MILL VALLEY: Record Shack; SAUSALITO: The Tides.

LEE CONKLIN

by Walter Medeiros

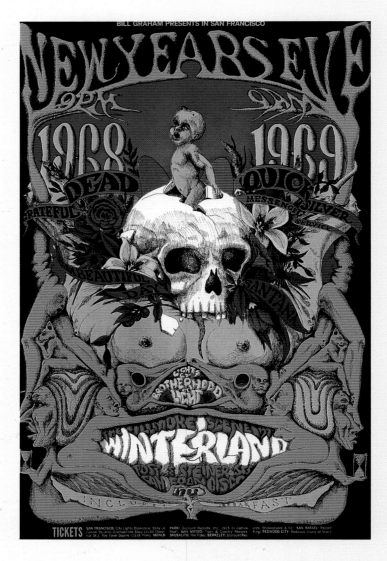

After Bonnie MacLean, Lee Conklin was the next artist to produce a large body of work for the Fillmore. He designed about three dozen posters, most of them during 1968. Conklin now lives in New York and background information has not been obtained, but it's apparent that he is a prolific and imaginative draftsman and very involved in psychedelic consciousness. At first Conklin's art may be hard to take for reasons of its weird imagery and also its style of drawing. The earlier draftsmen established an elegant standard; their drawing is neat and precise, and if the forms are complex they are at least rendered with strong, harmonious linework. Conklin works in a looser, more sketchy style, and his drawings are not immediately pleasing, either to the eye or the mind. But once past the initial resistance one may feel toward the style and the bizarre imagery, Conklin's art can provide both instruction and delight.

The lack of conventional harmony in Conklin's forms derives from his basic approach to drawing.

Generally, his is the art of detail; forms grow out of other forms and he accepts the grotesque result. This can be seen quite clearly in the rendering of the word "spirit" in one Jeff Beck poster. The crude proportions, outlines, and three-dimensional shapes of the letters derive from the fact that they are resultant forms, part of a figure-ground illusion.

Conklin can draw more precisely when he wants to, and in a variety of techniques. And he certainly doesn't stint on his labour, as the poster with the background mosaic of faces most clearly demonstrates. Even here his organic form-within-form process can be seen in the several larger faces which emerge from the background.

This personal psychedelic technique and imagery dominates Conklin's art, but occasionally he worked in a more conventional poster format. Several designs, especially his early ones, are quite clear and readable. One of these is based on the standard Wilson figure-upon-lettering format, and others contain imagery derived from band names. His invention is always remarkable and sometimes amusing; his motorcycle-satyrs are a delightful addition to the mythological bestiary. Conklin's designs are often entertaining as puzzles. Three-dimensional forms dominate his art, but several

⌂ New Year's
Eve Party poster,
Winterland, Lee
Conklin – 1968
BG 152

↺ Creedence
Clearwater Revival,
Fillmore Auditorium,
Lee Conklin – 1968
BG 127

⤴ Blues Bash,
Fillmore Auditorium,
Lee Conklin – 1968
BG 128

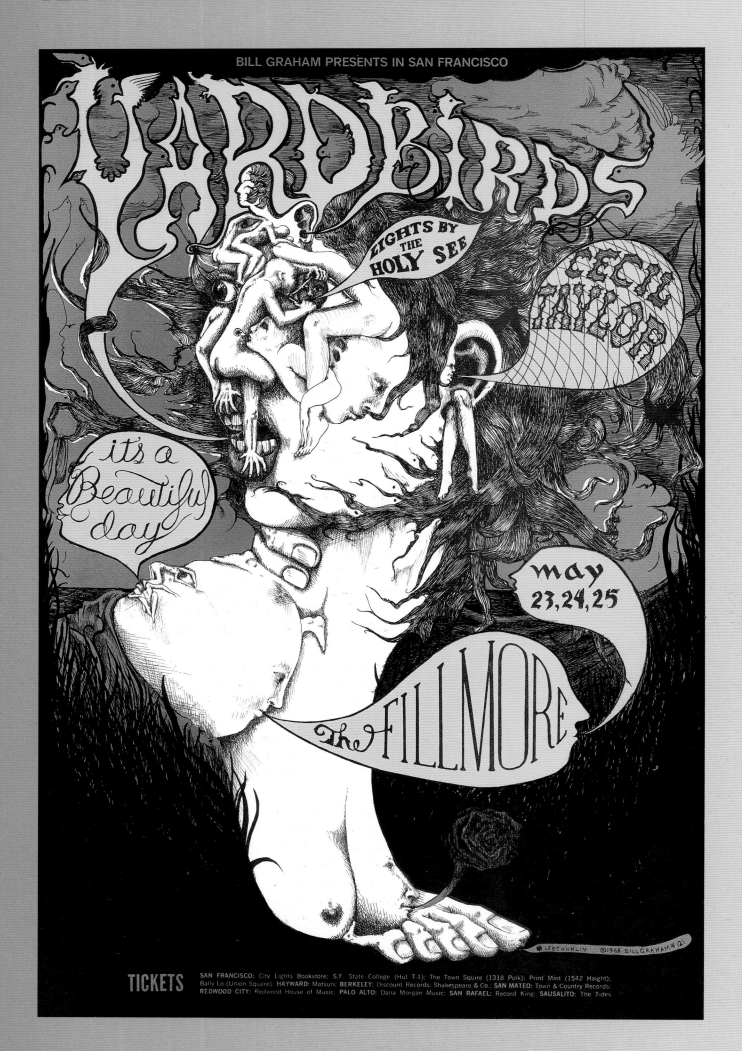

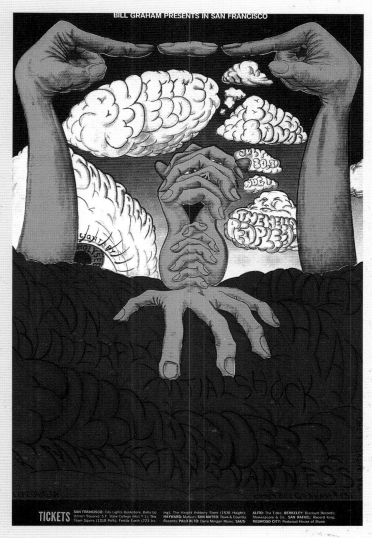

of his flat designs are among his best, and it is in these that his graphic illusions are most subtle. His seemingly inexhaustible capacity to interrelate forms undoubtedly derives from psychedelic experience and in these the results appear as a more intense version of an old form of a child's puzzle. This more conventional format tends to make the illegibility of these posters acceptable.

Conklin's stimulated imagination and tireless hand rang endless changes on the human figure. One design presents the figure as furniture, but the forms are usually organic. Even the earth comes to life; landscapes are common, there is a stalagmite figure, and an animal-vegetable-mineral figure that might have been inspired by one of Rick Griffin's designs.

The head is a favourite subject, too, and there are several designs which treat it in a monumental fashion. Psychedelic experience appears to be the most important influence in Conklin's art, but these heads suggest an additional source of his bizarre assemblage art; or at least they serve to link his art to a tradition. The grotesque visual pun of the human head composed of diverse objects, such as flowers, vegetables, armour or tools can be traced back at least four hundred years in European art. If one comes to appreciate the style of Conklin's art only belatedly, it is perhaps because art has traditionally presented the positive vision – harmonious form and noble, ideal beauty. And underlying that is the strong human tendency to avoid the unpleasant, including the visually grotesque. But weirdness is out there in real life, as well as in some levels of psychedelic vision, and in art it has a long tradition. What's more, it can be good graphic fun. © *Walter Medeiros 1976*

🎧 Butterfield Blues Band, Fillmore Auditorium, Lee Conklin – 1968 BG 131

🎧 Cream, Winterland and Fillmore Auditorium, Lee Conklin – 1968 BG 109

🎧 The Yardbirds, Fillmore Auditorium, Lee Conklin – 1968 BG 121

THE TEMPTATION OF EVE

EAST TOTEM WEST (1967-1968)

Joseph McHugh founded East Totem West with a talented group of local artists in the San Francisco Bay Area. He began with the premise that the poster normally employed to advertise travel or a concert announcement could find its place in the field of art. The major contributing artists to East Totem West were all experienced artists who had been schooled in a solid art tradition. Nick and Barbara Nickolds, Joe and Irene McHugh, Wilfried Sätty, Phil Bird and John Hamilton all contributed to enhance this new art form, the poster as art.

Premises were found on Throckmorton Street in Mill Valley, where a storefront was found that would serve as a gallery and retail outlet, with a warehouse facility to accommodate the mainstream, mail order side of things. Of all the East Totem West artists, Sätty became the most world-famous, and after the demise of East Totem West in 1968, went on to publish his own work as well as illustrating the works of Edgar Allen Poe and Bram Stoker's *Dracula*.

☾ 'The Temptation Of Eve', John Hamilton – 1967'

☽ 'Ancient Dance', East Totem West, Sätty – 1970

🎧 Wilfried Sätty – 1967

PHOTO: GENE ANTHONY

↷ 'Flapping Your Arms Can
Be Flying', Joe McHugh – 1967

☋ 'Mirage', Sätty for
East Totem West – 1968

↺ 'Fool On The Hill', Sätty
for East Totem West – 1967

☋ 'Cheshire Cat',
Joe McHugh – 1967

↻ 'Stone Garden', Sätty
for East Totem West – 1968

STONE GARDEN

© EAST TOTEM WEST, 550 Throckmorton Ave., Mill Valley, California 94941

THE AMERICAN SCENE : EAST TOTEM WEST

FUNKY FEATURES

Funky Features opened in 1967 as a poster print shop on Haight Street in San Francisco. The three owner-artists were known as "Funky Paul", "Funky Sam" and "Funky Jack". They became well-known for their psychedelic Zodiac series of posters, including themes influenced by William Blake, Aubrey Beardsley and Tibetan mandalas. The vast majority of their posters were intentionally designed to be seen under "black light" (ultraviolet), which caused the colours to leap into life.

↺ 'The White Rabbit In Wonderland', overprint, Joe McHugh for East Totem West – 1967

↻ 'Sunshine Man', East Totem West – 1967

↻ 'Psychedelic Cat', black light poster, Funky Features – 1967

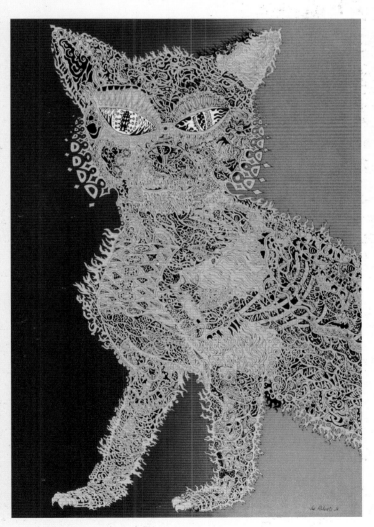

SUMMING UP

by Walter Medeiros

☾ 'A Day In The Life', Paul Olsen for Funky Features – 1967

☽ 'Buddha', black light poster, Funky Features – 1967

Local newspapers and journals began reporting on the art in late 1966 and national coverage soon followed. In the summer of 1967 *Life* magazine did a seven-page article on "The Great Poster Wave" which included photos of Wilson, Mouse, Moscoso and Griffin posed among their art, and began: "Suddenly posters are the national hang-up. They serve as low-cost paintings, do-it-yourself wallpaper, comic Valentines or propaganda for such things as *Batman* and rye bread. Posters in every dimension and description, from playing card size to billboard blowups, are being plastered across the US. More than a million a week are gobbled up by avid visual maniacs who apparently abhor a void." Filling the void, indeed. The expansive hippie aesthetic of "more" had already begun its surge over the clean norms of fashion and behaviour, from costume and interior decoration to drop-out lifestyles.

Personality posters, the enlarged photos of movie stars and other cultural heroes, had been popular for several years but it was the San Francisco art which created the poster craze. The graphic style of the rock posters also became popular within and without the rock culture. A lot of mediocre art was generated. but also some excellent poster artists developed around the music centres of America, some of whom modelled their art on that of one or another of the San Francisco artists. And like the music, the art went overseas: London had a poster scene and local posters were seen on walls in Europe and Australia.

In straight commercial art it was primarily the brilliant patterns and dense lettering – derived from Wilson's style – which were adopted. These elements became the stereotype of "turned on" graphic art. Bright pattern, diluted from its psychedelic origin, was useful in projecting that happy, expansive mood which supposedly stimulates consumers, and the unreadable lettering was, of course, straightened out a bit for less interested eyes. It took a couple of years but eventually these forms were commonly seen in public print, mostly in the ads of newspapers and light periodicals, but also in sober professional journals. In 1968 Wes Wilson was commissioned to design the programme cover for the convention of the Operational Research Society of America's Technical Institute of Military Science. He designed for them a woman in the shape of a cross.

Apart from the music world, aspects of the style survive in numerous, often minimal, forms. The most direct legacy is the several typeface designs which are modelled on Wilson's lettering. These are found in typographer's catalogues and also in the press-on letters sold in art supply shops. Also, the catalogues of these typeface suppliers are much richer in quantity and

ᯑ '‌Artist Rights Today',
benefit posters

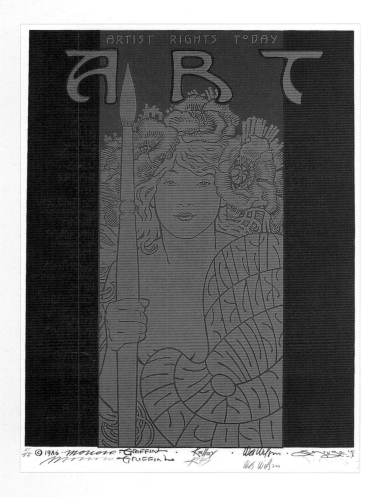

in decorative quality than they were a decade ago. But graphic art is no longer primarily a matter of selecting typefaces to enhance a photograph. Out of the poster craze has come a renewed interest in graphic art, its use and development, from lettering design to airbrush technique.

The impact of the poster art is perhaps more evident in the Bay Area, where its visual education was greatest. Derivative lettering styles commonly appear on the handbills which still grow in thick layers on the walls of Berkeley's Telegraph Avenue. The ads of Bay Area newspapers, primarily the weeklies and advertising monthlies, abound with examples of simple but sophisticated graphics. Within the past year, San Francisco billboards advertised the Ice Follies upside down and the Giants baseball team in backward lettering. The ripples of artistic freedom appear in more distant and lofty places, too. In the recently adopted title for their special reports, NBC News has sanctioned the graphic levity of mixing upper and lower case letters in the word "special".

Back in the late 1960s, from out of a sense of protectiveness of their newly-attained cultural identity, some hippies responded to the adoption of their art style by the straight world with jealousy and cries of "rip-off". Of course, some of it was – the world of commerce is always ready to exploit whatever is marketable. But on another level hippie art forms were simply appreciated and the adoption of the rock poster style by other artists was merely another phase in the process of expansion, of the general desire and readiness to find new ways of expression and fulfilment, the same consciousness which initiated the counterculture. It was also a continuation of the historical process of cultural interaction. The eclecticism of the hippie artists coming full round, the underground feeding back into the mainstream – how natural and proper and perfect. Change – interaction, duality, mutual arising – recognition and acceptance of this principle was one of the major lessons internalised by intelligent and sensitive hippies. You can hear that in the music and see it in the poster art.

Those were heavy times, in fun and otherwise – it wasn't all flowers. The poster art is a record of consciousness, and much of it reflects the hippies' basic assumption of the strong link between art and life. Art was for fun but also a medium of personal expression, an open connection to the human family. In 1967 Allen Ginsberg, explaining how his famous poem of the previous decade, 'Howl', began as a private "looking into the heart" went on to say: "[Jack] Kerouac put me on to the discovery that we're stepping forth into a time of irrevocable statement: speak now or forever hold thy peace. And then I realised that the exact area which is classic art and which everybody is interested in is just that – our secret personal doodlings. Art is something discovered from your own real nature." © *Walter Medeiros 1976*

SWINGING LONDON

It is generally acknowledged that the British "scene" and consequent eruption of psychedelia in England really began in the early summer of 1965 when Allen Ginsberg visited London and held a series of impromptu poetry readings. In June, he held a "standing room only" reading at Better Books, a small Soho bookshop that almost overnight became the Mecca of London's avant garde and Beat generation.

Ginsberg had already been exposed to London's hip scene through his public association with Bob Dylan and William Burroughs. More and more kids at the time were being energised by the *On The Road* lifestyle memorialised by Jack Kerouac's fictional intergalactic hitchhikers.

The mod style had given way to the gospel of Dylan, and protest was in the air. Out went the mohair suits and carefully groomed looks, and in came boxcar denims. Ginsberg was anxious to mount a poetry reading on a large scale to showcase the emerging American poets, many of whom were living in Paris and other European locations. The search for a venue began as increasing numbers of American performance poets agreed to attend and participate.

The Royal Albert Hall was finally chosen and booked, but now many British poets demanded to be represented. The reading was set for 11 June 1965. Ginsberg, Gregory Corso, Lawrence Ferlinghetti, Michael Horowitz, Andre Veznesensky were present, together with anti-psychiatrist RD Laing and his band of psychotic flower children. The guests were greeted at the doors by flower maidens who handed a bloom to each entrant. Indira Ghandi attended as Allen Ginsberg's guest. Barry Miles handed out sugar cubes. Wine, pot and incense flowed throughout the vast auditorium, and the bonding which took place

🎧 *Oz* magazine
cover – 1967

🎧 'Saville Theatre',
Hapshash And The
Coloured Coat – 1967
OAS 4

🎧 'Julie Felix',
Hapshash And The
Coloured Coat – 1968
OA 134

🎧 'Position 70', *Oz*
supplement – 1967

at this event cemented the core of the emerging British underground movement.

Later in the year, Michael Hollingshead returned to London after a spell at Timothy Leary's Millbrook New York mansion, equipped with LSD literature and more than 6,000 doses of acid. His avowed intention and mission was to "dose" (with LSD)[1] as many powerful people on the scene as possible, and with some further help and direction from Leary, he opened the World Psychedelic Centre (WPC). It was located in Pont Street, Chelsea, an up-scale section of London. Visitors to the Centre

staggered along until it was closed after the inevitable police "bust" in January 1966. Hollingshead was arrested and eventually served twenty-one months in prison for possession of hashish.

In that same year The Beatles issued their pre-psychedelic *Revolver* LP, and the scene exploded as the streets of London seemed to light up almost overnight. Colourful posters advertising the cosmic events of the week started to appear in Soho, Notting Hill Gate and Hampstead. Nineteen-sixty-six also saw the opening of such psychedelic era institutions as the *International Times*, the UFO Club as well as Indica Books.

🎧 'Move At The UFO Club', Hapshash And The Coloured Coat – 1967 OA 107

🎵 '14-Hour Technicolor Dream', International Times Benefit, Alexandra Palace, Michael McInnerney – 1967

🎵🎵 Record promotional flyer for 'Tomorrow', Jacob And The Coloured Coat – 1967

🎵 UFO Club Poster, Hapshash And The Coloured Coat OA 104

included William Burroughs, Roman Polanski, Eric Clapton, Hugh Hefner and Paul McCartney.

The demise of the WPC was inevitable. Although attended by many rock stars and media moguls of the day, the Centre soon faltered, largely due to Hollingshead's chronic behaviour problems which characteristically arose after he had consumed massive doses of acid, DMT and speed. In his autobiography *The Man Who Turned On The World*, he described first turning on Timothy Leary to LSD in 1961, and how the WPC

Of particular note were the dance and concert events at the UFO. Joe Boyd, an American born in Boston in 1942, had been working at the time for the UK branch of Elektra records. He joined with photojournalist John "Hoppy" Hopkins and Barry Miles in an effort to secure a location in which to hold further events akin to the spontaneous Roundhouse happenings. They found appropriate premises at the Blarney Club, 31 Tottenham Court Road, and secured a lease to hold events there beginning at 11:00 pm after the Irish Dancers had vacated the basement premises. The club, which was renamed only on Friday nights as the "UFO", remained open until 5:00 am.

The first of these events was called "UFO Presents Night Tripper". UFO served as a free form event, allowing poets, dance troupes and musicians to basically "do their own thing" encouraging spontaneity and impromptu performances. Pink Floyd, Soft Machine, Tomorrow, Crazy World Of

1: Within the LSD subculture there have often been those who thought it appropriate to place a measure of the substance in other people's food or drink without warning, sometimes as a form of practical joke and in other instances out of a messianic fervour to bring the acid experience to the uninitiated regardless of whether the recipient had expressed a wish to experience it

Arthur Brown and Jimi Hendrix were a few of the artists who appeared at UFO. Michael English was employed to create the Day-Glo posters which advertised these events, the first of which was held in December 1966.

After a series of "spontaneous" underground events held at the Marquee Club, groups like Pink Floyd, Soft Machine and Tomorrow effectively became the creators of the new psychedelic sound. These musicians and many other groups developed their skills in the warm glow of UFO's basement home, and the public's appreciation of their efforts grew in equal proportion.

In October 1966, the culmination of the year's events took place with the publication of the inaugural edition of the *International Times*, Britain and Europe's first underground tabloid newspaper. The event was celebrated with a party at London's Roundhouse, a beautiful old turn-of-the-century steam engine cleaning shed with a magnificent coned roof.

The Pink Floyd and Soft Machine provided the musical ambience at the event which was attended by an estimated 2,000 people, most of whom were in fancy dress. Sugar cubes were handed out at the door, Marianne Faithfull wore a nun's habit mini-dress style and Paul McCartney arrived looking like a crazed Arab, as the media stood by hardly able to comprehend what appeared to them to be a scene of complete madness. The poster on the outside wall proclaimed "*International Times* First All Night Rave Pop Op Costume Masque Drag Ball, et al. Bring Your Own Poison". The cutting-edge ambience of that evening was perhaps best illustrated by the Soft Machine's use of a microphone attached to a motorcycle's cylinder head, which was revved up from time to time to enhance their performance. The following John Platt[1] article elaborates:

○ 'UFO At The Roundhouse', Martin Sharp – 1967

C 'UFO Club', Michael McInnerney – 1967

CC 'Pink Floyd, UFO Club', Hapshash And The Coloured Coat – 1967 OA 114

1: John Platt: author, broadcaster, Sixties archivist, TV and film consultant, music and film researcher

"Prior to the autumn of 1966, there had been virtually no pop or rock posters in England that could be remotely described as artistic. Most were in the time-honoured boxing style, mainly of interest for the artists listed rather than having any intrinsic aesthetic value. The chief exception is The Who's 'Maximum R & B' poster – with its stark black and white image of Townshend whirling his arm and its imaginative use of lettering that was designed for their residency at the Marquee Club in 1965.

"Much less well-known is a series of crude but interesting posters from late '65 and early '66 done for the four Ricky Tick clubs scattered around suburban west London. These were never intended for sale and are, thus, incredibly rare. A variant of one of them, however, was later printed up and sold as a 'personality poster'. It features a head shot of John Mayall (in black and white)

🎧 'Sex',
Martin Sharp – 1967

🎧 'Max The
Birdman Ernst',
Martin Sharp – 1967

🎧🎧 'Plant A Flower
Child', Oz magazine,
Martin Sharp – 1967

with his name spelled out in quasi-Wes Wilson lettering over his face. There is no mention of venues or dates.

"Although the world of art failed to impinge on the minds of gig promoters, art and rock had been mixing in other ways. From the late Fifties a group of artists, including Peter Blake, Richard Smith and Joe Tilson (collectively known as Pop Artists, despite their lack of stylistic kinship with the American group of that name) began to draw on aspects of popular culture for their themes. Blake, in particular, was obsessed with Americana and rock music and over the following years produced 'homages' to Elvis, Chuck Berry and The Beach Boys. (He would later, of course, design the *Sergeant Pepper* album cover.)

"By 1963 the art schools were turning out students who had learnt from Blake and co and were ready to revolutionise

design in England. Fashion – especially in the emergent Carnaby Street – advertising, packaging and even TV shows (the seminal *Ready Steady Go* pop show plagiarised the work of artists like Blake and Derek Boshier for their set designs) began to display the influence of Pop Art. Whether the Brits knew it or not, much of the style of 'Swinging London' came out of the art world. One of the truisms about Sixties rock in England is that most of the musicians went to art school. It should be borne in mind, though, that most were enrolled because of the liberal atmosphere and any influence 'art' had on them was minimal (except for their clothes). An honourable exception was Pete Townshend, who has commented that the pioneer of auto-destructive art, Gustav Metzger, inspired his guitar-smashing binges. In any case, The Who came as close as it was possible to get, both visually and sonically, to a total Pop Art style.

"Pop Art and pop music were, almost by definition, contemporary, happening and NOW, but from about 1965 an

element of nostalgia began to creep in, as it did in San Francisco. Initially, it was the camp charm of Victoriana – the Portobello Road antique market became overrun with hip young people searching out old junk – but in short order the once-reviled styles of the Pre-Raphaelites and Art Nouveau became serious contenders in the world of genuine antiques. Likewise, with increasing numbers of people having had their horizons expanded by dope, it was inevitable that the visionary artists of the past, like William Blake and Samuel Palmer, would become fashionable. Similarly, the work of the divinely decadent Aubrey Beardsley was re-discovered, especially after an enormously influential retrospective of his work was held at London's Victoria and Albert Museum in the summer of 1966. Also brought out of the closet were the beautiful Edwardian books featuring colour plates by illustrators like Arthur Rackham and Edmund Dulac, with their fairy tale castles inhabited by elves, goblins and princesses. What was needed was a style that incorporated the old and the new and, perhaps, an excuse to produce the synthesis." © *John Platt, Psychedelic Poster Art In Britain*

Steve Stollman, an American intellectual who had helped produce the highly successful Albert Hall poetry reading which had been organised by Allen Ginsberg, chose to remain in London to create and organise additional "spontaneous" underground events. On Sunday afternoons, the previously unknown music group Pink Floyd made their debut at the Marquee Club, complete with primitive light shows and special effects. John Hopkins, Barry Miles, Peter Jenner and Andrew King came together at these events under the watchful eye of Robert Fraser, a wealthy Chelsea art dealer and friend of The Beatles.

↻ Oz magazine promotional poster, Martin Sharp – 1967

↻ Jimi Hendrix Experience, Ricky Tick Club – 1966

Peter Jenner, a lecturer in economics at the London School of Economics ("LSE") joined Andrew King to manage The Pink Floyd. Jenner, together with John Hopkins and Rhaunie Laslett, with the support of Michael X, also opened the London Free School in Notting Hill Gate. Established as a self-help community project with a wider political agenda, the Free School staged two benefits at the All Saints Hall in Notting Hill where once again The Pink Floyd were the host band, and liquid light shows were first introduced to the scene.

Oz magazine, the brainchild of Richard Neville was launched in early 1967. Neville had produced *Oz* while still living in Australia, and with partners Felix Dennis and Jim Anderson, had arrived in London with a bright, colourful, sassy magazine. Using overprinting in colour for the first time, *Oz* addressed social and political issues head-on, petitioning the British government on many issues and encouraging open debate on subjects which included drugs, sex, war and peace, as well as offering underground news and record reviews. Someone at the time was reported to say that if the *International Times* was the tabloid of the self-styled alternative society, *Oz* soon became its colour supplement.

↻ 'Hung On You', King's
Road Boutique, Hapshash
And The Coloured Coat
– **1967** OA 115

🎧 Soft Machine, 'Turn On'
record promo, Hapshash
And The Coloured Coat
– **1967** OA 101

The soon-to-become-famous poster artist, Martin Sharp, an old friend of Neville's, was employed as Art Director and artist in residence. He set about designing covers for Neville, of which 'Blowing In The Mind' advertising Bob Dylan was his most memorable.

By the autumn of 1966, the previously disparate parts of the underground movement had started to coalesce. One focal point was England's first underground newspaper, *International Times*, the launch party for which was held at the legendary Roundhouse in north London and featured the psychedelic delights of The Soft Machine and The Pink Floyd. John "Hoppy" Hopkins, Barry Miles and Joe Boyd needed no excuse to produce posters that would advertise UFO in a style that reflected the tastes of the time along with the nature of the club and its music. More or less.

In fact, part of the reason they decided to do posters was because they'd heard that the Avalon and Fillmore had them, and it sounded like a good idea. Michael English, one of the designers on the nascent *IT*, offered to do the artwork. Although harbouring a fondness for the work of Beardsley and Mucha, English was actually more into "techno-futurism", and his early designs for UFO (December 1966 through March 1967) while interesting, are a long way from the hallucinogenic swirls of genuine psychedelia. However, he was interested in breaking away from traditional type case and breaking into not only free-form imagery but also a more organic style of lettering, amply demonstrated by the giant pink Day-Glo lips that form the central design of the UFO Love Festival poster (10 February 1967).

In early '67 Michael English was introduced to Nigel Waymouth and the two agreed to work together. Unlike English, Waymouth was not a trained artist, in fact, at the time, he was proprietor of Granny Takes A Trip, the hippest clothing store in town, located on the fashionable King's Road in Chelsea. Waymouth, as he himself later put it, "had a keen eye" and, more to the point, was totally into Art Nouveau and fairytale art and was able to bring out those things in English's work. As English recalled in *3D Eye* (the book of his work):

"I was fascinated by the sinuous yet romantic shapes found in Mucha's posters and the work of Beardsley and Rackham. Meeting Nigel brought this to life; I responded to his romanticism. All [our] underground posters are packed with secret signs, prehistoric forms and flying saucers. We believed and adopted anything that contradicted the rational world: our science was rooted in alchemy and black magic.

↻ 'A Million Volt Rave At The Roundhouse' – 1966

↻ 'A Million Volt Rave At The Roundhouse' – 1966

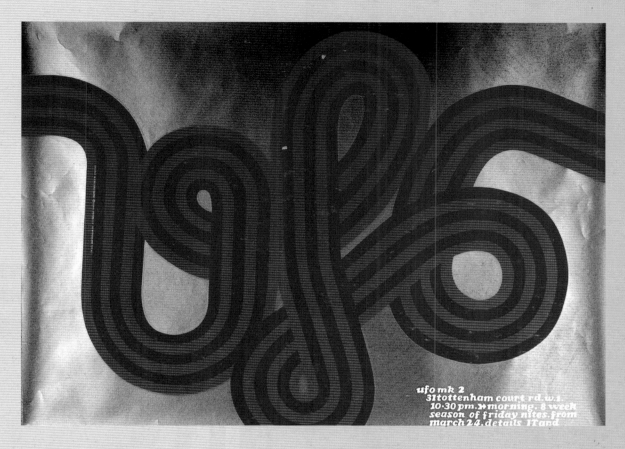

ufo mk 2
31tottenham court rd.w.1.
10·30 pm.→morning. 8 week
season of friday nites.from
march 24. details if and

🎧 UFO Club,
Michael English
– 1966

⮑ The Move,
Marquee Club,
Hapshash And The
Coloured Coat
– 1967 OA 109

Sexuality too was a strong force, and there is a lot of that happening in the posters. Dragons and pubic hair!"

The two initially worked under the name "Cosmic Colours" but produced only one known poster as such – the promo poster for The Purple Gang's record, the appropriately named, 'Granny Takes A Trip'. The duo subsequently changed their name to "Jacob And The Coloured Coat" and produced another one-off (the 'Luv Me' poster) before they settled, around March 1967, on "Hapshash And The Coloured Coat", the name by which they are best known. Hapshash, by the way, is a corruption of the name of the Egyptian queen, Hatshepsut. Over the next eighteen months or so they designed some of the most dazzling, beautiful and original psychedelic posters – as good as anything produced in San Francisco, LA or Detroit.

The two worked as a sympathetic team, each adding to the other's work until the poster was finished. The posters were silkscreened and the artwork for each colour was transferred to its own individual screen, then the elements

➲ Hendrix at the Fillmore Auditorium, Hapshash And The Coloured Coat – 1967 OA 103

↻ Cannabis Legalisation Rally 'The Putting Together Of The Heads', Hyde Park, Martin Sharp – 1967

☾☽ Record promotional poster for 'Art', What's That Sound – 1967 OA 113

☽ The Who, 'I Can See For Miles', record promo, Hapshash And The Coloured Coat – 1967 OA 123

of the image were married together in the printing process. In the same interview English commented, "We developed our own technique of putting two or three colours onto the screen, merging them together as the squeegee was pulled across. That was our most successful innovation."

The use of metallic and fluorescent inks created extraordinary effects and, in the case of some posters (notably the one for The 14-Hour Technicolor Dream) they changed the ink colours during the actual printing process, resulting in a huge number of variants within the one print run.

Around the time that English and Waymouth began working together, *IT* formed an offshoot company to handle UFO's posters and others. That they were to produce UFO posters was not a great surprise, since UFO, *IT* and the new company, Osiris Visions, were all, basically, run by the same people. (For some reason, a few of the posters credit it as Osiris Agency.) Although Hapshash produced the bulk of the Osiris posters, they were not the only artists who worked for the company. Mike McInnerney, another *IT* staff member, produced around a half dozen, including one for UFO (10 July 1967) and one of two posters for the Legalise Pot Rally. His poster style was akin to, but slightly tamer than, Hapshash's and, good though they are, he is best remembered for some of his album sleeves, notably The Who's *Tommy*.

⤴ Hapshash And The Coloured Coat record promo – 1967 OA 401

⤵ 5th Dimension Club, Leicester, Hapshash And The Coloured Coat – 1967 OA 118

⤵⤵ Crazy World Of Arthur Brown, Hapshash And The Coloured Coat – 1967 OA 108

More original than McInnerney and every bit as talented as Hapshash was Martin Sharp. An Australian, he'd come to Britain with Richard Neville the founder of Britain's second underground paper, *Oz*. Both had worked on the Australian *Oz*. The English version of *Oz* prided itself on its graphic design and set standards that have rarely been surpassed. Some of Sharp's *Oz* covers (notably his Dylan

"Blowing In The Mind") were turned into posters by *Oz*'s own poster company, Big O, and are amongst the best examples of British psychedelic art. Sharp's one Osiris poster for UFO at the Roundhouse, 22/29 September 1967 (after UFO lost their West End premises) is best described by reference to his cover for Cream's *Wheels Of Fire* album, to which it is stylistically related. Sharp's other posters (of which there were, sadly, very few) were generally in a unique collage style and printed on a metallic-faced stock-gold or silver. All of them were published by Big O. The rock related ones, including Donovan/Sunshine Superman, Cream and one for the Legalise Pot Rally ('The

They were agitated
by the drum.
The four Bacabs ride
on the back of a green
rainbow
one by one the stars fall

Putting Together Of The Heads') are amongst the best and most sought after of British psychedelic posters. Incidentally, Big O also turned a couple of Hapshash's *Oz* covers into posters 'Catherine And The Wheel Of Fire' and one sometimes called 'Position 70'. (Both are reproduced in *3D Eye* page 32.)

Osiris lasted until the late autumn of 1966, by which time the public taste for psychedelia in all its forms had dwindled to virtually nothing. People still wanted posters but rather than weird, freaky and arty, they wanted personality photo posters. In fact, a number of the later Osiris posters were of this sort, as was the bulk of the Big O catalogue. But at least their version of personality posters were of people like Che Guevara, rather than, say, tennis stars.

Although other British rock posters exist from the period, none were of anything like the artistic quality of the best of

artists only created them when the spirit moved. Whatever the reason, there is no consistent body of posters for UFO as there was for the Avalon or the Fillmore.

In the winter of 1967, Hapshash did a series of four posters for the Saville, a theatre on London's Shaftesbury Avenue. At the beginning of the year, Brian Epstein had leased the place for a series of adventurous Sunday evening concerts that featured many of the upcoming underground bands, as well as semi-established acts like Jimi Hendrix and Cream. If nothing else the shows gave those unable or unwilling to brave the uncompromising atmosphere of an all-nighter at UFO a chance to see the new bands. Why Hapshash were asked to do just four posters some nine months after the first show is unknown. Also curious is the fact that although all four are in the classic Hapshash style they seem a little cruder than

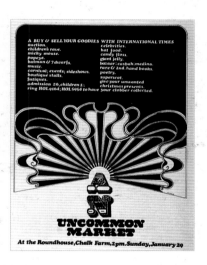

🎧 'Friday? Good!', Michael English – 1966

🎧 'The Purple Gang', record promo for Granny Takes A Trip, Cosmic Colours – 1967

🎧🎧 Intrenational Times, 'Uncommon Market', Roundhouse – 1966

🎧 'Tomorrow', record promo for My White Bicycle, Jacob And The Coloured Coat – 1967 OA 102

the Osiris series. The majority of the non-Osiris posters were designed almost purely for advertising purposes with no thought of art. Conversely, one wonders how seriously Osiris took the advertising aspects. A glance at the Osiris list reveals that although UFO operated almost every week for a year, there are no more than ten posters for the venue. Some, admittedly, announced upcoming events covering two weeks or more, but that still leaves gaps of many weeks when no posters were produced at all, and the only advertising was through ads in the press. Maybe they couldn't afford to do them at certain times, or perhaps the

the others and appear rushed. Maybe Epstein offered them huge amounts of cash provided they came up with the finished designs overnight.

Aside from the UFO and Saville posters, all the other gig posters are one-offs. There is one for the 5th Dimension, a regional rock club, located in Leicester, and one for a Move show at the Marquee. Others may be found on the list, but a few anomalies should be pointed out here: both Hapshash and Mike McInnerney produced posters for The 14-Hour Technicolor Dream, a grand event that took place on 29 April at Alexandra Palace in north London and featured over forty bands. Its purpose was to raise money for *IT*, who had recently been busted by the police for alleged obscenity. Despite the obvious connections with *IT*, no copy of either poster known to me mentions Osiris, or carries an OA number.[1]

Slightly less strange, but still odd, is the Hapshash Middle Earth poster. Middle Earth was another London

1: See section on Collecting Psychedelic Posters, page 163

↻ 'Middle Earth Club', Hapshash
And The Coloured Coat – 1968

↻ Michael English, Nigel Waymouth
and Guy Stevens – 1967

psychedelic venue that opened a few months after UFO but lasted a year beyond UFO's untimely demise, in October 1967. The one Hapshash Middle Earth poster – indeed the only real poster known to exist for the venue – covers most of March and April 1968, and it's one of Waymouth and English's best. Again, however, no known copies carry any reference to Osiris.

The existence of unnumbered posters raises another issue, ie the fact that some posters in the series exist both with and without numbers, or Osiris credits. My best guess at the moment is that in some (many?) cases the first run of a poster – the ones actually used to promote a gig, or used as genuine publicity, as in the case of the record company promo posters – does not have numbers, these being added on a second print run. This second and larger run produced posters that went on sale. Equally possible is that Osiris was staffed by stoned hippies who simply forgot, sometimes, to add the credits. In any case, the Osiris numbering system seems wilfully wayward at the best of times, so anything is possible.

THE OSIRIS VISION OF JOE BOYD

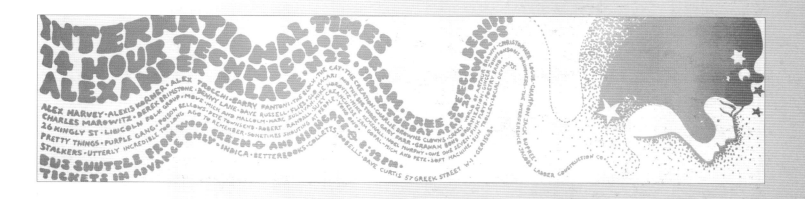

↺ Granny Takes A Trip
Boutique, advertising poster,
King's Road – 1967 OA 602

🎧 Flyer for The
14-Hour Technicolor
Dream

It was The Incredible String Band that brought Joe Boyd to my attention. I was a great fan and enjoyed their acoustic style.

Boyd was born in 1942 in Boston, Massachusetts and grew up there. He came to London with Elektra Records, and met the "Incredibles" and The Pink Floyd. Through those associations he met John "Hoppy" Hopkins. Hopkins and Boyd put their heads together to form the UFO Club. Boyd had already experienced the Family Dog and Bill Graham, and gave a sort of American sophistication to the UFO set-up.

Boyd and Hopkins needed posters to advertise their club, and both knew artists who were working in London. It was through them that two of the most respected poster artists of the time – Michael English and Nigel Waymouth – were introduced to form Hapshash And The Coloured Coat.

Joe Boyd formed Osiris Vision as a UFO poster outlet, producing some of the rarest posters of the period, culminating in a commission, direct from Jimi Hendrix, to design the poster for his upcoming show at the Fillmore East Auditorium in New York City. Although Osiris only lasted a mere nine months, they designed no fewer than fifty-seven posters. Joe Boyd now serves as Managing Director for Rykodisc Europe.

POSTER ARTISTS : MICHAEL ENGLISH

Born in Oxford, England in 1941, Michael English emerged onto the British psychedelic scene after completing art courses at Hammersmith School of Art and Ealing College of Art. In 1962, he befriended Pete Townshend who stimulated his interest in music.

After a brief stint in an advertising studio as a commercial artist, English broke loose and decided to go it alone. One of his earliest commissions was the 'Hung On You' shop front design, now a collectible poster. In 1966, English met Nigel Waymouth, who was also working on a shop front design for the King's Road's famous Granny Takes A Trip.

Michael had already worked in the paste-up room of the *International Times*, which had launched the UFO in December. Michael designed and printed the first UFO poster, 'Night Tripper', published in black and white to advertise the coming-out of the London underground. Subsequent posters designed by Michael English were silkscreened, using Day-Glo colours and incorporating English's distinctive lettering.

In early 1967, Michael English and Nigel Waymouth joined to form the design team Hapshash And The Coloured Coat. They continued to produce posters together for Osiris Vision, Joe Boyd's UFO printing company. In 1969, English produced a series of airbrush drawings which revealed more of his awesome talent, including 'Rubbish', 'Kinetic Ford', 'Coke', 'SW' and 'Shoe'. In the same year he held his first one-man art exhibition at the Motif Gallery in

↻ 'Welcome Cosmic Visitors', Hapshash And The Coloured Coat – 1967 OA 106

↪ International Times supplement, 'Summer Sadness For John Hopkins', Michael English – 1967

London. In 1967, English gave an interview about his work and the scene for the Ealing Art College magazine. This interview is most revealing, because it remains one of the few contemporary insights into the work of these artists.

"My first year at Ealing was a psychedelic experience – we broke away from normal channels of so-called education, we broke down everything to raw, bare essentials. We became quite primitive, till we knew a totally different way of expressing ourselves – it was mind expanding." This attitude was carried over into every part of his life.

"Scenes took place in a cafe over the road, where the groundcourse took over the juke box. We used to feed it shilling after shilling – just listening to records by Ray Charles, Booker T And The MGs and Barrett Strong – it blew my mind and everybody else. One day I walked in and – Zamm! – it hit me. 'Green Onions' was playing; it was so beautiful I just collapsed on the floor."

Life continued, however, moving from Fine Art to graphics; developing a personal culture; "Just listening to sounds, getting high and drawing – this helped to form my mind."

When he left Ealing he joined Masius Wynne Williams but after a few months left them, "to bum around and meet people.

"To my amazement other people were doing the same thing. Then slowly these scenes began to build up. It was like

➲ 'Luv Me' Film Productions,
Jacob And The Coloured
Coat – 1967 OA 301

guerrilla warfare tactics – pockets of resistance developing everywhere.

"Suddenly all these separate scenes began to emerge together and became one gigantic scene. It's growing fast and getting a lot of publicity."

Mike English is anti Victorian-type authorities who, he says, "have a false father complex – false because real people are forever children. Our society should be split into smaller tribes. Computers will become our hope. They will enable us to look within ourselves and become more creative."

In a recent interview English recalled:

"We were working from a studio in Holland Park, west London, where I lived in the flat above, we shared ideas and designs – he'd paint a bit and I'd paint a bit." This was where they produced the romantic Art Nouveau-influenced designs that became their trademark. Using three-screen prints with metallic inks, a series of posters were produced for Saville Theatre, as well as posters for regional music venues and head shops. A well-known head shop poster 'Welcome Cosmic Visitors' remains one of English's favourites.

Working continually for two years English and Waymouth parted amicably in the late 1960s to pursue their solo careers and as English now says: "I wanted to move away from symbolism and into reality." Turning his back on the psychedelic dream, English produced a space story comic book, which to this day remains unpublished and unseen having been bequeathed to his son.

During the 1970s having mastered the art of the airbrush, English produced a series on the theme "Rubbish", painting household items and foods. This hugely successful series of prints were published as large format prints in a Limited Edition.

English has for the past ten years worked as a graphic artist for companies worldwide and from his south west London studio remains as busy as ever. Quietly spoken and meditative, he recalls the Hapshash days and the thrill of receiving the commission for the 'Red Indian', Jimi Hendrix, Fillmore Auditorium poster which he describes as "chaos locked together with fluid Art Nouveau shapes": the nights spent at the Speakeasy club watching Jimi Hendrix jam on stage, his UFO club days, and the record the Hapshash duo made, produced by Guy Stevens, and made in an EMI studio hired for the night when everybody and anybody were invited to come along and perform, backed by The Heavy Metal Kids who later became Spooky Tooth.

English remains a great music enthusiast. Although somewhat more reclusive these day, he is a working artist who paints every day. His paintings hang in museums from New York to Canberra, as well as in private collections across the globe. He now describes his style as abstract, spiritual and once again symbolistic.

NIGEL WAYMOUTH

☾ OAS 3 ☽ OAS 2 ☽ OAS 1
Saville Theatre posters,
Hapshash And The
Coloured Coat – 1967

 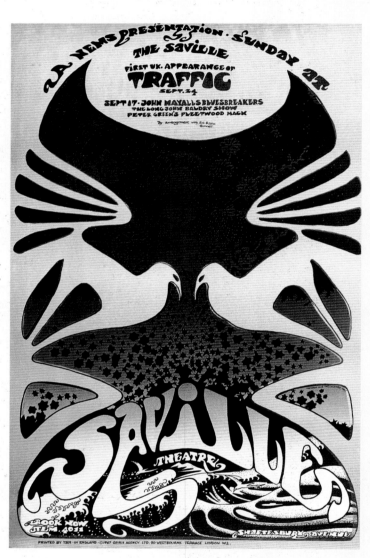

Nigel Waymouth was born in Kasauli, India in 1941. He studied economics at University College, London from 1960-1964. In 1966, he designed the shop front for Granny Takes A Trip located in the King's Road, London in collaboration with his then girlfriend Sheila Troy and John Pearse. He was a part owner of the shop.

Inspired by Aubrey Beardsley, Marvel Comics and Oscar Wilde, the shop clothed the hip and famous. The idea of Granny's was to change the shop front frequently. They had no difficulty in doing so with Waymouth's constant flood of design ideas, the most famous of which being the 1947 Dodge sedan coming out of the shop window.

Nigel Waymouth met Michael English in 1966 and they jointly designed posters for the UFO Club under the name "Hapshash And The Coloured Coat" until the group's demise in 1968.

↻ Legalise Pot Rally,
Michael McInnerney
– 1967 OA 105

MICHAEL McINNERNEY

Printed by TSR Printing & Publicity Services Ltd.

Born in Liverpool in 1944, Michael McInnerney moved to London in 1952 at the age of sixteen. From the late 1950s to the mid 1960s, after graduating from the London College of Printing, he met Michael X and John Hopkins. Hopkins invited him to join *International Times* in the autumn of 1966 as Art Editor, where he worked until it was closed by the Obscene Publications Squad in 1967.

A benefit for *IT* was organised for which McInnerney created the poster and helped with publicity. After the benefit, The 14-Hour Technicolor Dream at Alexandra Palace, he worked producing posters for Osiris and *Oz* magazine. It was at this time, through an interest in Meher Baba, that he met Dudley Edwards, and formed the legendary design team "Omtentacle".

Their first commission as Omtentacle was to design the shop front and interior for Pussy Weber's Flying Dragon Restaurant in the King's Road, Chelsea. After the success of this venture, they went on to design one of the most important psychedelic posters of all time, 'La Fenêtre Rose'. It depicted a tree, with a huge mass of Medusa-like hair as branches, offset printed in blue, gold and brown, advertising the Palais de Sports event featuring Spencer Davis, Cat Stevens, Dantalion's Chariot and Soft Machine. After the concert, the producers failed to pay the printers for the posters, who consequently destroyed all of the remaining stock. As Dudley Edwards explained, "The general practice in those days was to print a percentage for the billboards, and the rest went for distribution to the alternative underground shops." Consequently these posters are extremely rare, as few are known to exist.

McInnerney has continued his artistic pursuits, holding several one man exhibitions as well as creating, with Tony Wright, what many consider to be some of the best modern LP covers. His 1993 publication *Nova* features a retrospective of his work.

MARTIN SHARP

Martin Sharp was born in Sydney, Australia in 1942. He arrived in London after completing an overland trip from Singapore. With his keen interest in art and music composing, his creativity was well-suited for the happening London scene. Sharp frequented the Speakeasy Club, a favourite watering hole of London's rock elite. It was there that he first met Eric Clapton, who had just formed the band Cream. Sharp and Clapton became almost inseparable, so much so that Sharp moved into Clapton's King's Road residence.

The influence that Sharp had on Clapton was noticeable. He not only designed the cover art for *Disraeli Gears* and *Wheels Of Fire*, the two most prominent psychedelic album covers of the period, but he also wrote the lyrics for 'Tales Of Brave Ulysses' with Clapton for the *Disraeli Gears* LP.

It is reported that Sharp's studio was a dangerous place to be due to the amounts of LSD lying around. Eric Clapton soon changed, his hair was worn in an "afro", his clothes became paisley, and his guitars were transformed from the original finish to Day-Glo.

At this time Martin Sharp designed posters for the UFO Club as well as illustrating for *Oz* magazine. He was commissioned by Paladin Books to design the cover for the British publication of Timothy Leary's *Politics Of Ecstasy*. He was also commissioned by the Big O Posters to work on a series of transparent posters silk-screened in translucent colours on clear vinyl acetate, titled 'Smartiples'. These, together with the earlier foil posters, comprise the most important artworks to come from Big O studios. Martin Sharp designed for both Osiris Vision and Big O poster companies.

In 1969 Martin returned to Australia, setting up residency in the old Clune Galleries. Thelma Clune, the Director, had decided to sell the building. There was no rush for the sale however, and under the watchful eye of mutual friend "Charlie" Brown, Martin presented his first exhibition after his return. This was followed by The Incredible Shrinking Exhibition which comprised photographs of the first show re-exhibited in small gem-like mirror frames. These two exhibitions laid the foundations for the "Yellow House", an unrealised dream mentioned by Vincent Van Gogh in a letter to his brother Theo about a house in the south, in the sun, filled with creativity. Although Vincent did not imagine his artists community would be so far south, the opportunity for realisation of the idea had arrived. Conceptual Art had emerged. Music and theatre along with film nights and total environment installations were encouraged and fulfilled. Martin produced a catalogue and co-ordinated the setting up of artists' spaces to be prepared for the spring show of 1971. The Yellow House was a milestone in the history of contemporary art in Australia and was retrospectively reviewed at the Art Gallery of New South Wales in 1990 coinciding with the centenary of Vincent Van Gogh's death in Auvers, France on the 29 July 1890.

�] 'Explosion',
Jimi Hendrix by
Martin Sharp – 1967

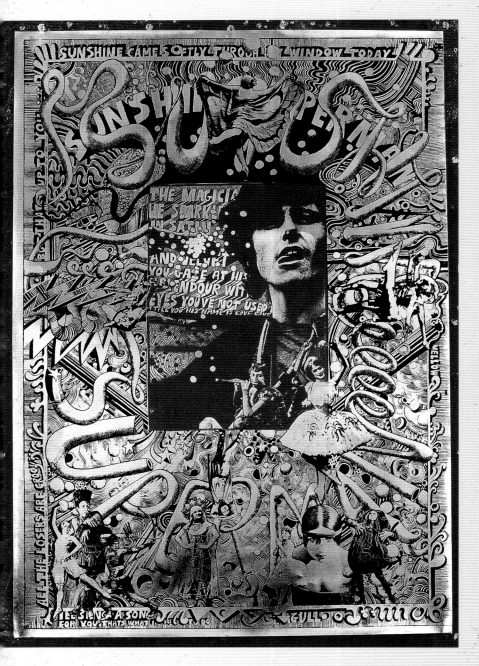

↺ 'Donovan,
Sunshine Superman',
Martin Sharp – 1967

↻ 'Cream',
Martin Sharp
– 1967

ing. Martin firmly believes the fire was an act of terrorism aimed at establishing alternative interests. Along with various other artist friends and sympathetic supporters, Martin was instrumental in forming The Friends Of Luna Park in an endeavour to remind the people of Sydney and the State Government of what they stood to lose if the site were developed. Martin's painting 'Snow Job' is a poignant reminder of his feelings about this matter, and if it had not been for the efforts of Martin Sharp, Sydney may have lost an important part of its character.

As well as Vincent Van Gogh, Tiny Tim remains one of Martin's strongest inspirations. Tiny's appropriation of song is very much like my appropriation of images. We are both collagists taking the elements of different epochs and mixing them to discover new relationships. Martin's appreciation of Tiny Tim has manifested itself in several ways – a five-metre painting now hanging in Macquarie University was painted during the mid Seventies with Tim Lewis. A film, *Street Of Dreams*, is described in Martin's painting 'Film Script'.

Although Martin has used most mediums available today he says, "It is only with acrylics that I am able to paint this way. The building up of the paint surface has not only given a new effect with paint, it is possible through acrylics to cover one colour with another providing changes to the colour resonance of the whole painting." For someone like Martin, who needs to tune his work to the highest possible octave, this is a distinct advantage – almost a necessity.

Like much of Martin's work this painting has to do with ideas, the intellect, refined composition and colour. What else would one expect from an artist whose influences are "the history of art", Vincent Van Gogh, Tiny Tim, icons of contemporary culture, the Bible, other great books, songs and more songs, and whose landscape is that of the imagination?

During the Seventies, Martin engaged with the Nimrod Theatre and produced the Nimrod posters. This important set of posters, now a collector's item like so many of his limited editions, included his poster for the play *Young Mo*. The Australian comic, *Mo* became the symbol of the Nimrod Theatre and one of Martin's most well known images. The subjects of Luna Park and Tiny Tim became Martin's other preoccupations during the Seventies. He was engaged as a designer and artist to oversee the restoration of Luna Park, including the commission to revamp the enormous laughing face at the entrance.

In 1979 a tragic fire in the Luna Park Ghost Train claimed seven lives, and silenced the optimism for a newly restored Fun Park. Martin's work on the Luna Park Face was ruined, and the park's theme, "Just for fun", lost its mean-

BIG O POSTER COMPANY

Bob Dylan, 'Blowing In The Mind', Martin Sharp for Big O – 1967

'Vincent', Martin Sharp – 1967

'Live Give Love', Martin Sharp and Michelangelo – 1967

Big O was conceived by Peter Ledeboer while he was a partner at *Oz* magazine. The great success of Martin Sharp's poster for the Legalise Cannabis Rally, held in the summer of 1967, convinced him that a poster company formed off the back of the notorious *Oz* magazine, with Martin Sharp as the vanguard artist, would be a money spinner. In August 1967, Big O opened up their shop. The 16 July poster for the Cannabis Rally, inspirationally printed on gold foil paper, was a definite hook for Big O Posters, and became an instant best seller along with other foil paper posters including 'Blowing In The Mind' (advertising Dylan) and 'Sunshine Superman'.

Big O eventually lost direction after Sharp's departure, producing commercial posters, which were not in step with the times, and attempting to sell them through their Carnaby Street outlet. However their fortunes revived and Big O was restored to its former glory as a result of a brief association with famed album cover artist Roger Dean, and a subsequent book titled *Views*.

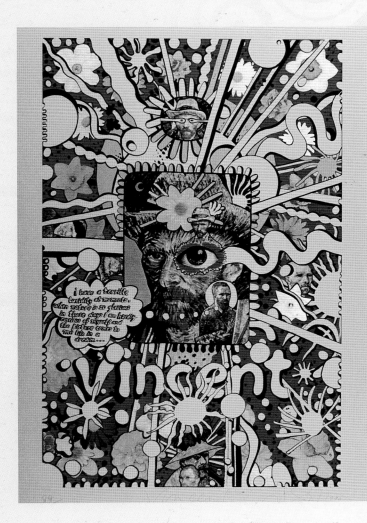

THE FOOL

This Dutch design team captured the hearts of psychedelic London, and The Beatles were heavily smitten by their imaginative work. They first came to prominence designing the album covers for one of the underground's favourite groups, The Incredible String Band, which was signed to Elektra records under Joe Boyd. The team fluctuated between three and four members, although the main artists were Marijke Koger, Jos Je Leeger and Simon Posthuma. They were often seen at UFO, and were also in attendance at major psychedelic events in London.

The Beatles commissioned them to design an enormous mural, as well as the interior for the Apple Boutique, occupying the entire corner at the intersection of Baker and Paddington Streets in central London. They also designed clothes for this Apple project.

➲ **The design team known as The Fool.**
PHOTO: ADAM RITCHIE
– 1967

➲ **'Love Bob Dylan',**
Marijke Koger – 1967

➲ **Album cover for The Incredible String Band designed by The Fool – 1967**

Their association with The Beatles led them to paint John Lennon's Rolls Royce in traditional Gypsy Caravan style with a psychedelic twist. Their relationship with Apple continued, with The Fool designing eight posters for the Boutique, as well as designing for the two Beatles films *Nowhereman* and *Magical Mystery Tour*. Other works included commissions from the groups Cream and Procol Harum.

☊ 'A Is For Apple' poster to promote The Beatles' shop in Baker Street. Designed by Simon and Marijke of The Fool – 1967

DAVID VAUGHAN

⟳ Psychedelic Buick
painted by David Vaughan.
Company car for design
team Binder, Edwards
And Vaughan – 1967

↻ Jean Shrimpton, 'Love',
David Vaughan – 1967

↻ Alan Aldridge – 1968

↻↻ 'Don't Look Back',
Alan Aldridge – 1967

David Vaughan was born in Manchester, England in 1944, and studied at the Ashton School of Art and Bradford Art College. He started his graphic design career by teaming up with Dudley Edwards and Douglas Binder, exhibiting their joint works at up-scale galleries in London in 1966. Vaughan painted the psychedelic Buick company car of the design team Binder, Edwards And Vaughan.

Vaughan was best known for his furniture designs, such as customising Paul McCartney's piano with fairground images. He went on to design murals for Dandy Fashions in the King's Road, Lord John in Carnaby Street, and the British Pavilion at Expo 67. Inspired by Martin Sharp and an association with fashion photographer David Bailey, he produced major contributions to psychedelic poster art. Like Sharp, Vaughan printed on metallic silver paper, eg the 'Buddha Single Head', 'Buddha Double Head' and Jean Shrimpton 'Love' works.

ALAN ALDRIDGE

Alan Aldridge, born in England in 1943, rose to prominence in the Sixties explosion of pop culture in Britain as the fiction Art Director for Penguin Books. Between 1963 and 1967, he brought a brash humour and fantasy vision to paperback art. In addition to his own surreal, often grotesque airbrush illustrations, he commissioned many strikingly original photographs taken in unusual locations and also produced a number of memorable covers for *The Sunday Times'* colour supplements during the 1960s and 1970s.

He edited and illustrated both volumes of *The Beatles' Illustrated Lyrics*, and was responsible, along with George Perry, for *The Penguin Book Of Comics* (1967). In the same year he created the poster for the Pennebaker film on Dylan, *Don't Look Back*. Since the 1970s, he has collaborated with airbrush artist Harry Willcock in designing and illustrating numerous children's books.

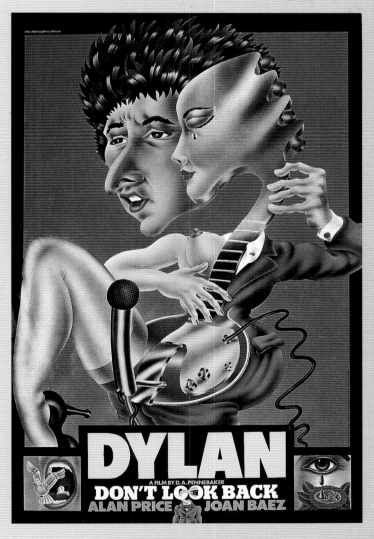

↻ 'Imagine', John Lennon by Alan Aldridge – 1967

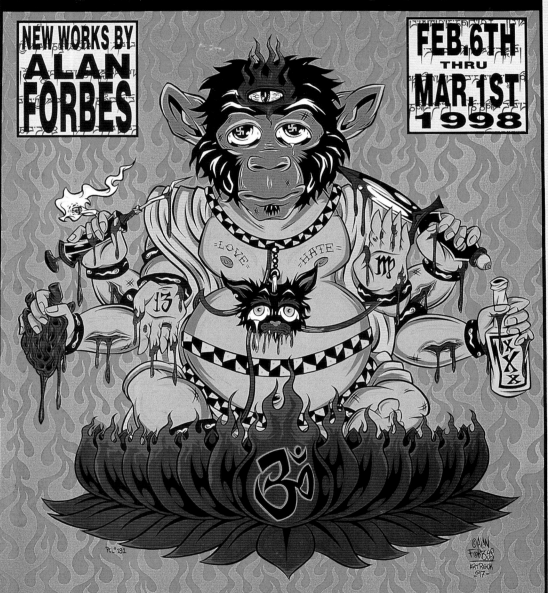

ALAN FORBES

↻ 'It All Went South',
La Luz de Jesus Gallery
show, Alan Forbes – 1998

↻ Mono Men,
Alan Forbes – 1998

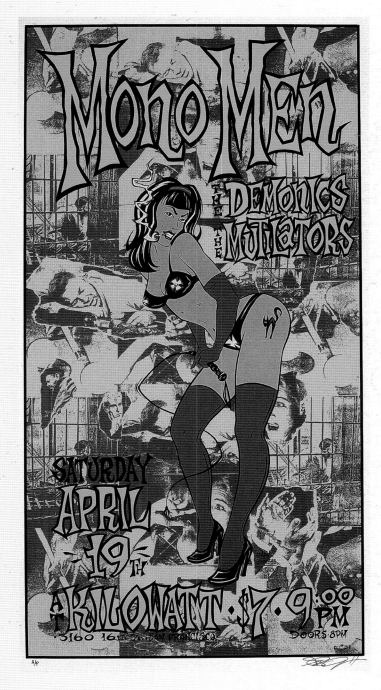

Some of the most charged and electrifying poster art of the Nineties spins from the mind and hands of San Francisco's Alan Forbes. His album covers and posters have been commissioned by such cutting edge rock groups as The Black Crowes, Rage Against The Machine and The Makers, while his paintings of found objects have been sold out prior to the openings of his gallery shows in Los Angeles and San Francisco.

Forbes was born in Connecticut into what he describes as an "eccentric family". He recalls that he was "shipped" to Los Angeles at the age of twelve, and during his teenage years he plunged deeply into the sex, drugs and rock 'n' roll atmosphere that surrounded him there.

He began his career as an artist by painting kitsch *objets d'art* which he found in second-hand stores. Utilising figures as diverse as old tikis, porcelain Dutch girls and ceramic Buddhas, Forbes covers them with representations of his own experiences, dreams and ironic humour wrapping around each piece until a new story is just starting or being told. He was able to start showing his found object paintings at Billy Shire's La Luz de Jesus Gallery in Los Angeles through the support and help of southern California artist Pizz (whose work is described by Forbes as "Hell unchained"). He also counts among his artistic influences the works of Robert Williams and Ed "Big Daddy" Roth.

After spending what he terms an "uninspiring" year in Santa Cruz, Forbes' move to San Francisco in late 1993 provided him with the opportunity to apply his painting skills and dramatic use of colour to the realm of psychedelic poster art. His poster art and paintings on found objects reflect his early street influences, as well as such varied and eclectic sources as images from early Sixties hot-rod and biker magazines, TV cartoons, alternative comics, terror-toy puppet monsters, *Mad* magazine, vintage and modern horror, monster and science fiction movies, tattoo shops, voodoo (from his alternative lifestyle parents), and recent forays into cubism and Hindu art and culture.

Forbes' art demonstrates his almost fanatical attention to detail, and despite his lack of formal art training, the technique and use of colour show a level of skill and sophistication well

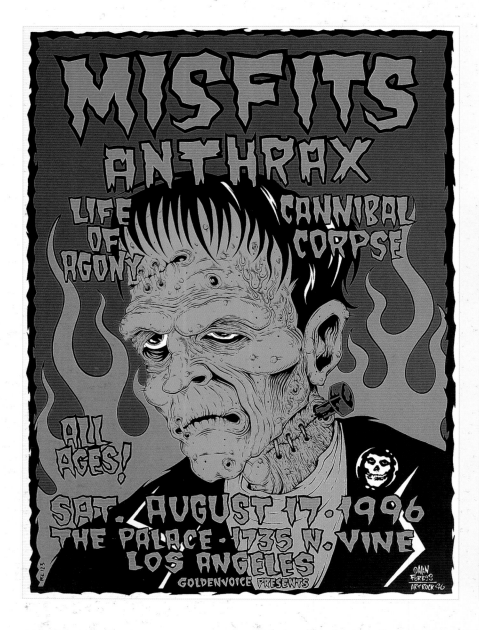

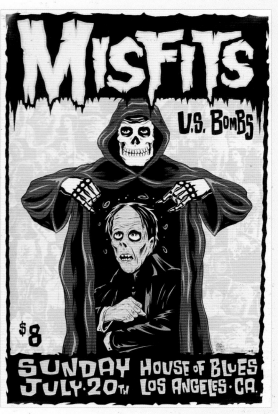

↻ Oblivians,
Alan Forbes – 1998

↺ Misfits and Anthrax,
Alan Forbes – 1998

↻ Misfits,
Alan Forbes – 1998

beyond his years. He also insists upon personal involvement in the silkscreen printing of his posters to achieve and maintain sharpness of form, contrast and brilliance of colour.

As mentioned, Forbes has created album covers and poster art for such groups as The Black Crowes, Rage Against The Machine, The Damned, Misfits and Reverend Horton Heat, and for musicians playing at important West Coast venues including the venerable Great American Music Hall and the exceedingly hip Bottom of the Hill (where Oasis appeared on their first American tour) in San Francisco, the Palace in Los Angeles, and Mercer Arena in Seattle. When asked by viewers to explain the meaning of imagery in his works of art, Forbes generally replies by inquiring what the questioner finds in the piece. "If they are able to articulate what they see, they have made the piece their own, and I won't argue."

He devotes equal time to his posters and painting, as he strives to push his efforts in each medium to another level. Forbes restricts the runs of his silkscreened posters to limited editions of 250-500, and they regularly sell out as soon as they become available. He has sold more than 150 of his found object paintings, and all of these pieces exhibited in his shows at galleries in Los Angeles and San Francisco since 1996 have sold out in advance of the opening. His art has been featured at gallery shows in Los Angeles, San Francisco and New York City, and Forbes is collected internationally.

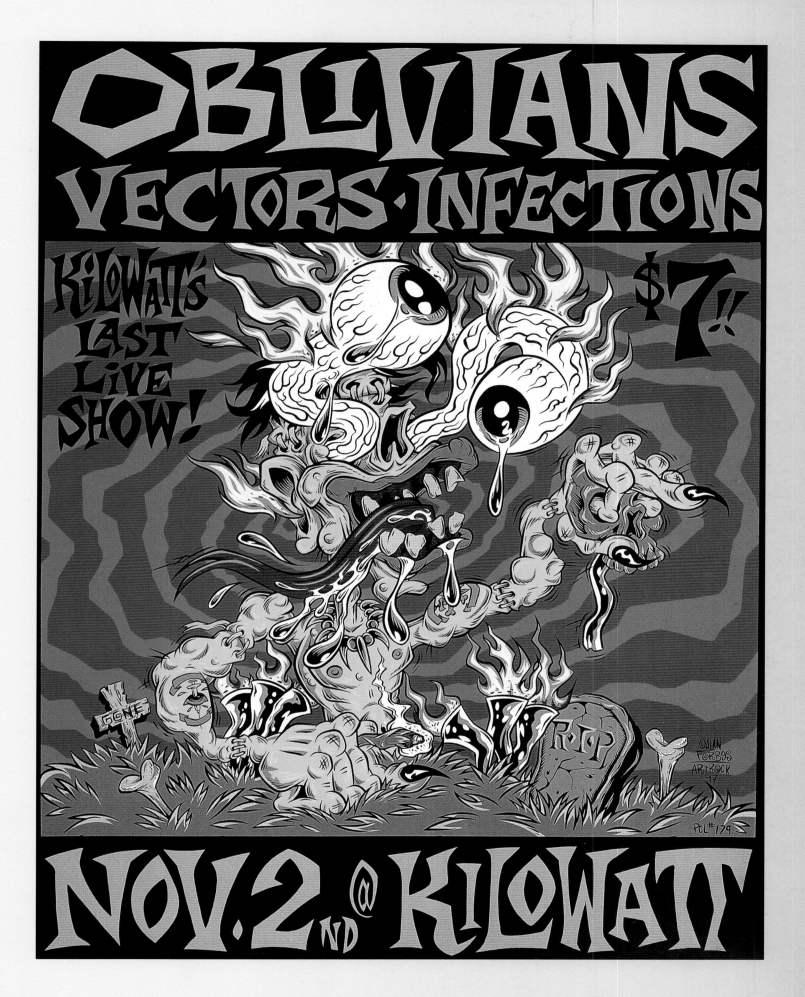

MARK ARMINSKI

↪ The Cramps,
Mark Arminski

Born in 1950, Mark Arminski, grew up in Detroit, Michigan like Stanley Mouse and Gary Grimshaw. While in high school during the mid-late 1960s, Arminski was creating his own psychedelic rock concert posters to show to his friends. These early efforts were considerably influenced by Grimshaw's Grande Ballroom posters.

Arminski initially studied art at the Oakland (Michigan) Community College, and from 1978-1979 was enrolled at Detroit's prestigious Centre for Creative Studies. His formal education also included the study of Stone Lithography at the Kalamazoo Institute of Arts, and at Dynamic Graphics Educational Foundation in Peoria, Illinois, where his courses were in computer-generated art.

Arminski's creation of modern psychedelic rock poster art really began in 1991, when he began to collaborate with poster printer Chris Dorris and his company, Ghetto Press. Over the next two years Arminski and Ghetto produced more than eighty posters, including those for local bands and such nationally recognised performers as Smashing Pumpkins and Iggy Pop.

Arminski's poster style features bold colour, strong central images and a whimsical sense of humour which helps connect the audience with the event. It appears to combine elements of the styles of the original Psychedelic Poster artists of the Sixties and Seventies, with the more graphic efforts seen in the works of such "new wave" Psychedelic Poster artists as Forbes and Kozik.

In 1994 he began producing a series of silkscreen posters, and related handbills for shows featuring such varied groups as Nine Inch Nails, Los Lobos, Stone Temple Pilots and Aerosmith at venues in Detroit and elsewhere throughout the United States, including Houston, Cleveland, and San Francisco. Although presently known nationally and internationally for his rock concert posters, he is not satisfied to be pigeon-holed into that one artform. Whether creating works as varied as murals for posh Motown bistros or doing a "performance" of body painting a living female model in the presence of cheering onlookers, Arminski is capable of moving comfortably in all artistic environments without pretension or loss of energy.

🎧 'Love Masters',
Mark Arminski

➲ Crash Test Dummies,
Mark Arminski

☮ Pantera, Mark Arminski

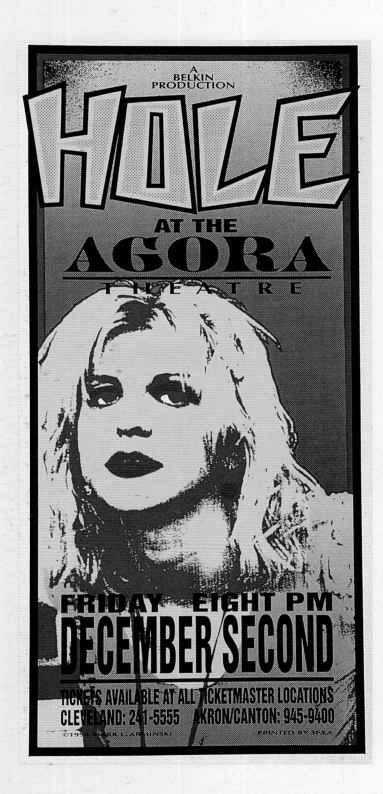

⌒ Tom Jones,
Mark Arminski

⌒ Hole,
Mark Arminski

Beastie Boys,
Frank Kozik

FRANK KOZIK

After growing up in Spain until the age of fifteen, Kozik emigrated to the United States in 1976. Living in Sacramento, California, he began soaking up American "trash culture" as exemplified by the comic book rock band Kiss, whom he saw perform at the Oakland Coliseum. In the early 1980s, while stationed in Austin, Texas to complete his four-year service commitment in the US Air Force, he started to attend shows at the city's hardcore punk rock clubs.

He drew his first rock poster in 1982, and over the next five years created another fifty of them, which he has characterised as "super crude"; however these works were the foundation upon which he developed the craft which subsequently resulted in world-wide fame. In 1987 he was living in a bleak suburb of Houston, working as a delivery truck driver. After breaking up with his girlfriend, he reportedly went out to the woods and tripped on Peyote, after which he decided to totally change his life. He immediately quit his job and returned to California to embark on his career as a poster artist.

Living in San Francisco, Kozik has created and produced numerous posters for musical artists of all genres, ranging from Boss Hog, White Zombie and Rocket From The Crypt to Nirvana, Pearl Jam, Green Day and Neil Young. His garishly coloured works utilise the shock value of contrasting such

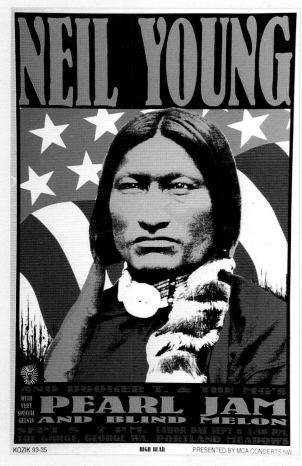

cute comic book characters as the Flintstones and Archie and Veronica with such negative cultural icons as Hitler and Charles Manson, and big-breasted women in disturbing poses. He has reportedly stated that, "My posters always garner a response. Whether it's positive or negative really doesn't matter. Shock value is good."

In the Nineties, Kozik has consistently produced more than 100 limited edition (300-500 each) silkscreened posters annually, and has also been commissioned by such mainstream patrons as Nike (which paid him to develop a European ad campaign). He currently distributes his posters through his merchandising company, Man's Ruin, and in the late Nineties has put major energy into the development of his record label of the same name, signing many new, cutting edge bands, and producing many records and videos.

↶ Neil Young,
The Gorge, Frank Kozik

↷ Jimi Hendrix,
Frank Kozik

↻ Soundgarden,
Frank Kozik

COOP

Chris Cooper, who publishes his art under the name "Coop", grew up in Bixby, Oklahoma where his early influences included *Mad* magazine, Hot Wheels toys, *Speed Racer* and other old Warner Bros cartoons. After first hearing The Ramones in concert as a teenager, Coop immersed himself in the punk rock scene, which in turn led him to discover underground comics and the brilliant work of Robert Williams.

Coop moved to Los Angeles aged nineteen, and began his career as an artist by creating album covers and illustrations for *Hustler* magazine. He has since focused on limited edition silkscreened rock show posters for such groups as Stone Temple Pilots, Foo Fighters, Rocket From The Crypt and Reverend Horton Heat.

As a follower of precepts of the late Anton LaVey, founder of the Church of Satan, devil images figure prominently in his work. His cover art for a Lords Of Acid album, *VooDoo You*, which depicted a pair of naked women, represented as succubi (female devils) engaged in graphic lesbian sex acts, became the catalyst for a national debate in America around pornography. These images of women who may not need men at all are often perceived as both disturbing and arousing by the viewer.

🎧 **Untitled, Coop**

↻ **The Jesus Lizard, Ministry, Coop**

↪ **Rocket From The Crypt, Whisky, Coop**

In what may appear a strange dichotomy, images in Coop's artwork reflect not only his interest in matters Satanic but also his ongoing passion for play. As reported in *Juxtapoz* magazine:

"Rows of amusement devices clog the square footage of Coop's combination working library/domicile/studio/garage. Notable deposits of Hot Wheels, Frankenstein figures, Shriner Fezes, rare vinyl discs, glamgirl men's mags, Hot Rod books, Rothabilia, skulls, robots and polychromed, lathe-turned bowling pins stand among thousands of collectible objects."

Coop also maintains that the music scene is also an important element in his art. This is a school of art that grew up out of listening to rock 'n' roll music and living that lifestyle. It's all grunge trash disposable culture. Yet it is his images of intimidating, powerful women who appear to be using their sexual wiles to lure innocent or weak men into their clutches, that has brought greatest public attention to Coop's work.

🎧 Boss Hogg, The Troubadour, Coop

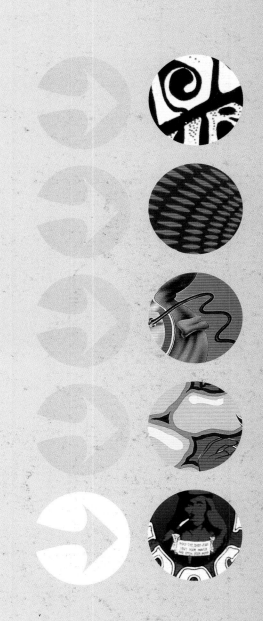

🎧🎧 Psychedelic art on
display at Bonhams'
1997 London auction,
organised by Ted Owen

COLLECTING PSYCHEDELIC POSTERS

by Alan Caplan

INTRODUCTION

This chapter is directed primarily at the novice collector, one who appreciates and relates to the beauty and excitement of psychedelic posters, but who has never owned one, or possesses only a few of them. However collectors of all levels of sophistication may benefit from the discussion of collecting strategies, review of available reference materials and a survey of sources for their buying and selling.

Although inexpensive reprints of vintage psychedelic posters are readily available, this discussion will focus primarily upon "original" period posters. This choice is not a function of price, but rather one of uniqueness and quality. Although the colours on reprints are often distorted, and the images less clear, their cost may not be much less than some of the newer, more exciting original posters. For example, there are excellent limited edition silkscreen posters created by emerging and skilful young artists like Alan Forbes, and printed by high quality print shops such as the San Francisco Art Lab, currently available for as little as £20-£25. Likewise, collectible, attractive concert posters, carefully produced by the "offset" printing method, and actually used to promote shows featuring major performing artists, may be available for even less money.

Two generic variables which may affect the artistic value and monetary price of psychedelic posters are the printing process (silkscreen or offset) which was employed, and the quality of the stock on which it was printed. In silkscreen printing, the image is imposed on a screen or other fine mesh, and the blank areas are coated with an imper-meable substance. The ink is then forced through the screen onto the print stock. In offset printing, the image is transferred indirectly by using a metal or paper plate to ink a smooth rubber cylinder that transfers the ink to the paper. Silkscreening, is very labour-intensive, and a slower and more delicate process than offset printing. Also, the maximum practical number of posters to a run in silkscreen printing is approximately 2,000, while with offset printing, there is no such limit.

Most of the available silkscreened psychedelic posters are done in six colours. That does not mean that there are only six colours shown; only that the artist and printer utilised five basic colour inks plus black, and the many other colours appearing on the poster were created by mixing them. There are rarely more than twenty-one colours used in even the most expensive silkscreen poster because each colour has to be printed separately as an overlay. To illustrate these points, in a six-colour poster a green might be fabricated by mixing a blue ink with a yellow ink; whereas in the twelve-colour, the artist might choose to find and include a green ink of the exact shade he wanted as a separate colour, and could still have the option of mixing it with other colours for still more subtle shadings. Thus the number of ink colours affects the poster's depth of colour and subtlety of shadings.

When I mention "Fine Art" prints, I am describing silkscreen prints with twelve colours, printed on the most expensive paper, and the limit on each run of these would be 500. Such Fine Art prints (depending upon theme, featured personalities and presence of signatures) usually retail for between $500 and $1,000.

Certain basic considerations, factors and concerns must be addressed whether you intend to acquire only a few psychedelic posters or to build an entire collection. They all impact to some degree upon the purchasing decision, and involve the interplay of the buyer's interests, motives and needs. These include:

Authenticity: It is crucial to ensure that each poster is exactly what the seller advertises and the buyer understands it to be.

Condition: The physical condition of a poster will clearly and directly impact upon its value, both visual and monetary.

Rarity: The availability of a poster greatly affects its price. Among the main considerations which affect the rarity of a poster are whether it was printed in limited numbers, and the extent of simple attrition (loss or destruction over the years).

Visual Artist: The identity of the visual artist who created it obviously impacts upon a poster's value. However the work of even well-known and collected artists may be devalued if they are so prolific that their works are too plentiful and generally available.

Performing Artist: The enduring popularity of a performing artist or group advertised in the poster directly and substantially affects its value. However this factor is a very subtle one, and is impacted by time. Even if a vacuous pop phenomenon such as The New Kids On The Block fills entire stadiums for a tour, the posters are unlikely to hold their value after such performers disappear from the public scene.

Venue and Date: These are highly important factors in determining a poster's merit. Works by the same visual and performing artists are likely to be more valuable if created for performances at such famous venues as London's Royal Albert Hall and San Francisco's Fillmore Auditorium. Likewise, a combination of age and historically important venue, such as the Avalon Ballroom in San Francisco and the UFO in London can increase its worth.

Signatures: The value of a poster is enhanced if it bears the authentic signatures of the visual artists or the performing artists. The extent of such increased value depends upon the importance of the signer and the rarity of such autographs.

Miscellaneous: Other factors impacting upon the price of a psychedelic poster (but not necessarily its true value) may include the seller's need for immediate cash or the exposure given to the item's availability (local, national, international). These may either lead to a bargain price for a rare poster, or a higher price for a comparatively ordinary one.

In this chapter I will first delve into each of the factors affecting the value of a poster in some detail. Then I will discuss goals for building a psychedelic poster collection (buying and selling), and strategies for achieving them. Finally, I will identify sources for the purchase and sale of posters. Throughout all of these discussions I will identify and review various reference materials and sources which are readily available to aid the collector. A basic principle which should always be kept in mind (in psychedelic poster collecting as in life) is that if any deal seems too good to be true, it probably is; therefore in most instances you should pass on it.

AUTHENTICITY

In determining the authenticity of a psychedelic poster there are many available resources, including descriptive books and the advice of other collectors and dealers. Perhaps the most important of these is really your own sound exercise of common sense. If a poster is being offered by a reputable seller who has been in business for a number of years, and the price is $100 or less, it probably is exactly as advertised. It simply would not be worth your time and energy to engage in extensive research.

A basic understanding of the technical meanings of certain words used by poster sellers and collectors is also a necessary element of self-protection. For example, a poster may truly be "original" and "vintage", but also merely a third printing. Many Fillmore series posters were initially printed in very small runs of 500-1,000 posters, and distributed before the shows which they advertised. Second and third printings (1,000-2,000 in each) of some posters were run off at the time of, or shortly after the show. Therefore you might see an advertisement for a 1968 Fillmore series poster for as little as £30, and it would be for an item which was actually produced in 1968, and would correctly be characterised as an "original" rather than a "reprint". However it would be of considerably less value than a "first printing" of that same poster.

You should also be aware of the recent trend of producing new psychedelic posters which "celebrate" or "commemorate" a past show or event. The posters may indeed be wholly psychedelic in form, and the brilliant creation of a major poster artist; however, they are certainly not "vintage". Therefore one must be cautious when considering certain carefully crafted advertisements which hint otherwise.

For example, a magnificently drawn poster issued to commemorate a 1969 performance by The Doors was described in a retail rock paraphernalia/memorabilia catalogue as having been "created by one of rock's most notable artists Randy Tuten, for The Doors' 24 January 1969 fantastic performance at Madison Square Garden". The truth is that the poster is very beautiful, and was in fact created by Randy Tuten who is among the greatest of psychedelic poster artists. However it was not produced "for" the show as indicated in the ad, but was drawn thirty years after the event. The misleading description was certainly not Randy's fault.

One final lesson may be drawn from the foregoing example. Although the catalogue writer clearly sought to convey the impression that this Doors poster was produced beforehand to advertise the show, it carried a retail price of only $14.95. Good old common sense would dictate that the price of a vintage poster for a 1969 show at an important venue like Madison Square Garden, headlined by a group as collectible as The Doors, would certainly be considerably higher. Therefore whilst it is truly excellent art, it would not be considered a "rare" or "vintage" poster. As I said, in poster collecting, as in life, you usually only get what you pay for, especially because so many experienced, sophisticated collectors have already ferreted-out and bought up for bargain amounts most of the available stashes.

An increasing trend in collecting psychedelic posters is that the seller may offer to provide the buyer of an item with a "certificate of authenticity". While in some instances this may be very useful, especially for resale in the future, you must consider the source of the guarantee, and what recourse you would have against the provider if the proffered certificate were to prove inaccurate. In some cases the certificate might prove of no more value than a "lifetime guarantee" from an off-brand manufacturer of a £20 wristwatch. If (or when) it fails, will the seller still exist, and even if it does, how likely is it that you will actually be able to obtain a new watch or your money back?

A letter or certificate from a reputable, knowledgeable and reliable source which guarantees the provenance of an item is certainly a valuable asset, both financially and to the extent that it provides the buyer with a measure of "peace of mind". However it is equally obvious that a certificate of authenticity is only as good as the authenticator who provides it. Therefore, before making a significant purchase in reliance upon such an assurance, take steps to verify the seller's background. Information such as how long the vendor has been in business, references from other customers, second opinions from other experts, and information about the vendor's source for the item would certainly be helpful.

There are also written reference materials available, which all serious collectors should personally possess. Among these are the magnificent 516-page, coffee table size book, *The Art Of Rock* by Paul D Grushkin (commonly referred to as "AOR"). It was published in 1987, and is truly considered the "Bible" of collectible rock 'n' roll posters. Carefully researched and documented, this brilliant work contains extensive discussions and representative photos covering the entire history of rock 'n' roll posters from 1955-1987, including pictures of most of the series posters from the Family Dog, original Fillmore, Grande Ballroom and Neon Rose. The book also is very usable as a research tool. Posters have been cross-indexed by visual artist, by performing artist(s) and by venue, and the reader has also been presented with an exhaustive bibliography.

Each poster photo in the *AOR* has been sequentially numbered, and among dealers and collectors the posters are frequently referred to either by series initials and chronological, sequential numbers, or by *AOR* plate number. Thus Family Dog posters are referred to by "FD (number)", and Bill Graham series posters by "BG (number)". Likewise, for example the traditional version of The Charlatans' famous early poster 'The Seed' would also be referred to as "AOR 2.1", and the original version as "AOR 2.2". Therefore you can always search the AOR to verify the existence of a proposed acquisition, and to determine whether it at least appears to be genuine.

Another essential resource for determining authenticity is *The Collector's Guide To Psychedelic Rock Concert Posters, Postcards And Handbills* by Eric King. It contains a detailed discussion of every poster, handbill and postcard in the Family Dog, Fillmore, Russ Gibb/Grande Ballroom and Neon Rose Series, including distinguishing features which differentiate the original and subsequent printings (if any) of each. Although "trainspotting" collectors and dealers sometimes grouse over a few of King's conclusions, any serious collector should own a copy of this work, which is frequently updated. Therefore, be sure that you obtain the most recent edition.

Coming back to the principle of using one's common sense, your need for exhaustive authentication will vary in direct proportion to the rarity and cost of your proposed acquisition, and an assessment of the honesty and reliability of the seller. If you are purchasing a first edition of all but the most rare posters, or a second or third printing of the series posters from a well-established retailer like Psychedelic Solutions in New York or Artrock in San Francisco, you can remain confident that you will receive exactly what was repre-

sented. On the other hand, if you intend to obtain a very rare or otherwise unusually expensive item from any source, you would be well-served to do some research on your own, or if enough money is at stake, it may be appropriate to seek an expert opinion as to its authenticity.

Another "authentication" concern relates to signatures on a poster. I am not aware of any substantial forging of the visual artists' signatures; however the genuineness of those by performing artists is a legitimate issue. The usual interplay of expenditure and risk would apply in this instance. That is, unless you are spending a large amount of money (say, £300) in specific reliance upon the authenticity of the signature, it would not be worth the time and expenditure to locate and pay an expert to verify it, especially if you are acquiring the poster from an established, apparently reputable source.

CONDITION

The "use your common sense" mantra should be applied in considering the importance and value of a poster's condition. Other factors being equal, certainly in any instance a "mint" condition copy of a psychedelic poster will be more valuable than a tattered one. On the other hand, a less than perfect copy which has been signed by the visual or performing artists may well be more valuable than an unsigned mint one.

The reference works discussed above will assist you by recounting the number of posters which were printed with each edition of the series posters, such as the Family Dog and Fillmore. If it is an extremely rare poster, and you believe that the price is a fair one, condition should not be a grave concern. Pin holes, tape markings and other evidence of the poster's use may detract from value if clean copies are read-

ily available. Yet it may also be an indication that the item truly was a vintage one, and not a recent forgery.

If you feel (at a gut level) that the poster seems cleaner than you might have expected for one of the advertised vintage, or if the stock on which it is printed just doesn't feel old enough, and you are being asked to spend a substantial sum of money to acquire it, further enquiry is clearly warranted. If the seller's explanation is simply that a previously unknown stash of mint condition rare posters has just been discovered, a second opinion would be appropriate.

RARITY

The term "rarity" in the context of psychedelic posters may refer either to those which were printed in limited numbers, or those which are not readily available to collectors in the marketplace. This distinction is based upon the fact that although some dealers have large reserves of many of the Family Dog and Fillmore series posters, they have been careful not to flood the market. Because mint condition, first printings of some of these "rare" posters certainly exist, the limited availability and high trading prices for such items is somewhat artificial.

Other facts which cause a poster to become rare include natural attrition over time (loss or destruction), and limited edition printing. The first printings of vintage posters from the late 1960s and early 1970s, whether from England or America, were often few in number (250-500). Because they were produced for the explicit purpose of advertising and promoting a show, they were tacked up on telephone poles, or taped to store windows. Many of these were simply thrown away after the show. Likewise, the young fans in their teens or twenties who took the free posters which were distributed at concerts, put them up on the walls of their bedrooms or apartments. As they grew older and left their parents' homes, dormitory rooms or shared living situations, the posters were often perceived as mere valueless pieces of paper, and were abandoned or destroyed. Fortunately for today's collectors, others were squirrelled away and kept for many years until their eventual release into the marketplace.

Although a psychedelic poster's rarity may be a highly important factor in determining its value, it is unlikely alone to be the crucial one. A poster which is ugly, or was created by an unknown visual artist, or which promoted a show by generally unknown performing artists, will not become desirable to collectors simply because it is a rare one.

Some posters are intentionally printed in limited, numbered editions to establish rarity and thereby enhance their value. Often these are silkscreened on fine paper, and almost invariably signed by the visual artist. If such variables as the identity of the poster's creation, the enduring popularity of the performer(s), and the location of the venue are essentially equal, the fact that a psychedelic poster is from a limited, numbered and signed edition will certainly make it more collectible.

One other factor which may cause an otherwise ordinary poster to become "rare" is if it has been signed by one or more of the performers whose names (group or individual) appear on it. Except for a few numbered, limited edition posters, they are not issued with the performing artists' signatures. Therefore, even an "ordinary" poster which has been signed by a performing artist will become "rare". The degree and value of such rarity will vary directly with the popularity and reputation of the performer, and the frequency with which the performer has been willing to autograph items.

VISUAL ARTIST

If you intend to build a substantial psychedelic poster collection, it is almost axiomatic that you include examples of works of all the well-known and acknowledged visual artists. Not only would such an approach be more aesthetically pleasing to viewers, it would also enhance the collection's value.

If you only intend to be a casual collector of a few posters, I suggest that you look around at posters of all kinds, consider the various factors which affect authenticity and value, and then simply buy what you like, regardless of who created it. Yet if you intend to spend a significant amount of money on a purchase, keep in mind that if a quick resale becomes necessary, it is more likely to occur if the piece was drawn by one of the famous artists.

The signature of the poster artist may enhance the value of a poster by as much as £25-50. Other facts being equal, a poster bearing the signature of a deceased artist like Rick Griffin will be worth more than the inscription of one of the still living artists, who generally will agree to sign their vintage posters in return for a modest fee. They frequently make appearances at rock 'n' roll memorabilia and posters shows for this purpose. If you contact them and are willing to pay for their fee and necessary postage, they are likely to be willing to sign and return any posters which you send to them.

PERFORMING ARTIST

The names of performing artists which appear on a psychedelic poster is obviously a vital component of its monetary value. Paradoxically, however, the mere fact that a poster advertises a performance by a group of legendary popularity (like The Rolling Stones) may be less valuable than a poster for a band with only a "cult following", like The Sex Pistols. The basic reason for this is that there are literally millions of pieces of Stones memorabilia out there, and only thousands from The Sex Pistols.

I certainly do not suggest that all Sex Pistols posters are more valuable than all from The Rolling Stones. It is simply that so very many Stones posters have been printed and distributed, that they have become readily available and not expensive to acquire. There are also a number of extremely rare Stones posters which carry prices far in excess of any from The Sex Pistols. These comparisons are given solely to serve as examples of the many considerations applicable to poster acquisition.

Whether you are a casual or serious collector, there is another important consideration in evaluating the impact of the performing artist upon a poster's value. You must exercise judgement as to whether the current popularity of the performer will continue at the same level. To choose some recent examples, consider The Spice Girls, Celine Dion and Mariah Carey. In the late 1990s, each was able to sell out stadium-size venues, and their memorabilia is presently fetching substantial prices in auctions and from dealers. Yet in terms of value, the issue becomes whether you can rely upon the proposition that if you buy a poster today, it can easily be resold at the same or greater price in the future. While you may enjoy the music today, ask yourself whether the performer's works will truly endure in the public consciousness? Simply put, are you dealing with a Bruce Springsteen or a Peter Frampton?

There are no simple answers to these questions. However if you consider an item's purchase price to be modest, and you like the poster as art, then your ability to dispose of it without monetary loss should not affect your decision about buying it. On the other hand, if you are paying a lot of money, ask yourself the hard questions, and be sure to be satisfied with the answers. Above all, don't act impulsively.

VENUE AND DATE

As with almost every other consideration in the collecting of psychedelic posters, the impact of a show's location and date upon its value can be the proverbial double-edged sword. Other things being equal, a poster for a show by an important performing artist will be more valuable if it was at one of the legendary venues such as the Royal Albert Hall, Roundhouse, UFO and Marquee Club in London, the Fillmore, Avalon and Winterland in San Francisco, or Detroit's Grande Ballroom. The series posters for the San Francisco venues, being frequently traded, have fairly well-established prices, and there is substantial availability of most of them if you are willing to pay the price.

In many instances, a poster on a particular date may be more valuable than an ordinary poster for that group and venue because that show is considered by the performer's fans to be particularly memorable. Other reasons why a poster for a particular show may be widely sought-after may be as varied as it being the first or last performance by a musician or group, or the final show before a performer died or a band broke up.

An entirely different theory employed by some collectors is that the most desirable and valuable posters are those for shows by major performing artists at highly obscure venues, especially when the major artist was not the featured act. Despite the fact that the art on such posters is generally inferior to that produced by the recognised psychedelic poster artists the rarity of these posters is what intrigues many sophisticated collectors. An example of this phenomenon was a small, orange and black poster for a show in the late 1960s at the University of California at Davis, at which the headliner was blues artist Big Mama Thornton, and the opening act was The Grateful Dead. The poster had lettering and a single colour photo of Big Mama, and the creator of the poster was not identified. Yet three years ago it sold for $1,500 at a poster show attended by leading collectors and dealers from all over America.

Posters from the famous venues of the 1960s where the names of such now legendary performers as The Beatles, Stones, Who, Cream, Elvis, Dylan and Grateful Dead appear at the bottom of the playbill, are also extremely rare. That is because they were generally simple, black and white, "boxer"-style posters, printed solely as advertising and without "artistic" concerns. Their purpose was simply to get the basic word out about the show, therefore they were usually thrown away immediately afterward. Also, before the groups became famous few people were interested in saving them as souvenirs.

OSIRIS VISIONS POSTER SERIES

by John Platt

This list was compiled primarily from the set of Osiris posters that had been the *IT* file set. These were donated to the Victoria and Albert Museum by Barry Miles, who also annotated them. Unfortunately, his set was not complete. Further information comes from my own researches and collection and that of Jack Wolffers (of Richard Wolffers Auctions, Inc, San Francisco), whose assistance has been invaluable.

It should be noted that Osiris started to number series and then abandoned them for no apparent reason. Osiris also ran some series concurrently. The posters are approximately thirty inches by twenty inches, unless otherwise stated.

Main references for this section:

Michael English: *3D Eye.* Paper Tiger, UK, 1979 (referred to as *3DI*).

Mick Farren, ed: *Get On Down.* Futura, UK, 1976 (referred to as *GOD*).

Pre-Osiris Work by Michael English:

Friday? Good! Silkscreen, 1966.
Drawing of The Last Supper in an oval frame.

Night Tripper. Offset, December 1966.
Photograph of girl's face (Karen Townshend, wife of Pete Townshend). First UFO poster.

UFO. 27 January 1967.
Oversized silkscreen.

UFO. 27 February 1967.
Oversized silkscreen.

Pre-Osiris Work by Cosmic Colours:

The Purple Gang/Granny Takes A Trip.
Offset, circa February 1967.

Promo poster for Transatlantic Records.
(*GOD* p24)

THE OSIRIS 100 SERIES

By **Hapshash And The Coloured Coat** and produced by silkscreen unless otherwise noted.

OA 101 *The Soft Machine Turns On.* Circa March 1967. Promo poster for the band. The number, "OA 101", was at some point used for 'The Move At UFO', which is most commonly found with the number, 1007 [yes, two zeros!]. See below, OA 107. (*3DI* 17, without the silver border; *GOD* 45)

OA 102 *Tomorrow/My White Bicycle.* Circa March 1967. Promo poster for Parlophone Records. There is another printing of this poster, probably an early state, that credits Jacob And The Coloured Coat rather than Hapshash And The Coloured Coat. The Jacob version is the one reproduced in *3DI.* (*GOD* 33, *3DI* 16)

OA 103 *Jimi Hendrix At The Fillmore Auditorium.* June 1967. Obviously, this is not an official Fillmore poster. Allegedly, Hendrix commissioned it himself. There is a very rare version of this (which may possibly be the earliest version) that omits the Fillmore details and, in the bottom right-hand corner, refers to the *Are You Experienced?* album with the Track Record logo and catalogue number. (*GOD* 39, *3DI* 16)

OA 104 *UFO Coming.* June 1967. (*GOD* 43, *3DI* 20)

OA 105 *Legalise Pot Rally.* Mike McInnerney. 16 July 1967. This poster exists in at least two versions. The early one lacks the "OA" number. (*GOD* 12, two-colour repro only)

OA 106 *Welcome Cosmic Visitors.* 1967. (*3DI* 32)

OA 107 *The Move At UFO.* 26 May 1967. At some point, there was a printing of this poster wherein the number is given as OA 101. More confusing is that on the more common version, the number is given as 1007, without an "OA" prefix. But 1007 seems to have been retrospectively reallocated as OA 107, at least in terms of Osiris's files. It is not known if any subsequent printings (if there were any) have OA 107 on the posters. To confuse things even further, a new version was created at the request of the band, wherein the UFO details were dropped and replaced with "The Move" in large psychedelic lettering, printed in silver. The only copy of this variant I have seen still has 1007 as the number. (*3DI* 21, *GOD* 13)

OA 108 *The Crazy World Of Arthur Brown.* 1967. An archetypal Day-Glo Hapshash poster, not to be confused with the various photo posters of Arthur Brown that Osiris subsequently published. (*GOD* 44, *3DI* 22)

OA 109 *The Move At The Marquee.* Michael English. 11 July 1967. (*GOD* 48)

OA 110 *UFO.* 10 July 1967. Mike McInnerney. (Does not appear in *GOD* or *3DI*)

OA 111 *Unknown.* Number may not have been allocated.

OA 112 *The Soft Machine Turns On.* Either a reprint or number reallocation of OA 101. See also OA 107.

OA 113 *Art/What's That Sound?* Circa May 1967. (Not in *GOD* or *3DI*)

OA 114 *CIA-UFO.* 28 July 1967. (*GOD* 40)

OA 115 *Hung On You.* 1967. Poster for a hip King's Road clothes boutique. Allegedly little used because it was unreadable. In fact, it was no more or less unreadable than any of the others. (Not in *GOD* or *3DI*)

OA 116 *Save Earth Now.* 1967. An early ecological poster. (*3DI* 24)

OA 117 *The Mothers Of Invention At The Royal Albert Hall.* Offset. 23 September 1967. (*GOD* 62)

OA 118 *5th Dimension, Leicester.* September 1967. (*3DI* 28, *GOD* 42)

OA 119 *Unknown.* Number may not have been allocated.

OA 120 *Dantalion's Chariot At The Roundhouse/UFO.* 22 September 1967. Martin Sharp. (*GOD* 41)

OA 121 *Jazz At The Roundhouse.* Mike McInnerney. Circa September 1967. (Not in *GOD* or *3DI*)

OA 122 *Unknown.* Number may not have been allocated.

OA 123 *The Who/I Can See For Miles.* Circa September 1967. Promo poster for Track Records. (*3DI* 27)

OA 124 *Richard Bernstein Exhibition, Amsterdam.* Circa October 1967. (Not in *GOD* or *3DI*)

OA 125 and **OA 126.** *Unknown.* Numbers may not have been allocated.

OA 127 *Incredible String Band At The Queen Elizabeth Hall.* Offset. 4 October 1967. (Not in *GOD* or *3DI*)

OA 128 *Unknown.* Number may not have been allocated.

OA 129 *Fairport Convention.* Gregory Irons. Circa December 1967. Promo poster for the band. (A black and white reproduction appears in Patrick Humphries' *Meet On The Ledge: A History Of Fairport Convention.* Eel Pie Publishing, London, 1982 p24.) The only known English poster by the San Francisco artist.

OA 130 and **OA 131.** *Unknown.* Numbers may not have been allocated.

OA 132 *Incredible String Band/Mystical Pantomimes.* March 1968. Tour poster, various venues. There is a recent bootleg of this poster, which is easy to distinguish from the original because the bootleggers have added The Doors to the bill (11). (*3DI* 26)

OA 133 *Unknown.* Number may not have been allocated.

OA 134 *Julie Felix At The Royal Albert Hall.* 18 April 1968. (*3DI* 23)

THE OSIRIS 200 SERIES

Silkscreen, unless otherwise noted.

OA 201 *UFO Love Festival.* Michael English. 10 February 1967. (*GOD* 25, *3DI* 16)

OA 202 *UFO MK 2.* Michael English. March 1967. (*GOD* 34)

It is believed there were only two posters in the 200 series.

THE OSIRIS 300 SERIES

OA 301 *Luv Me.* Jacob And The Coloured Coat. Silkscreen. 1967. Promo poster for Luv Me Film Productions Ltd. May also exist with a Hapshash credit. Also exists without an "OA" number. (*3DI* 19)

OA 302 and **OA 303.** *Unknown.* Numbers may not have been allocated.

OA 304 *Zappa On The Toilet.* Designer unknown. Offset. 1967. (Not in *GOD* or *3DI*)

OA 305 *Hendrix And The Move At The Royal Albert Hall.* Designer unknown. Offset. 14 November 1967. Basic design is a photo of elephants fucking. (Not in *GOD* or *3DI*)

OA 306 *Incredible String Band In Glasgow.* Designer unknown. Offset. Late '67 or early '68. Some copies say OA 3061. (Not in *GOD* or *3DI*)

OA 307 *Leap Year.* Designer unknown. Offset. 1968. Photo of naked black girl, leapfrogging over naked white boy. (Not in *GOD* or *3DI*)

SUNDAY AT THE SAVILLE (OAS) SERIES

All are by Hapshash And The Coloured Coat, and all are offset. Copies of all four also exist without numbers.

OAS 1 *Jimi Hendrix Experience (And Others).* 27 August 1967. (Appears in Mitch Mitchell and John Platt's *Inside The Experience,* St Martin's Press, New York, 1993 p79.)

OAS 2 *Traffic (And Others).* 17 September 1967. (Not in *GOD* or *3DI*)

OAS 3 *Unknown Acts.* 1 October 1967. (Not in *GOD* or *3DI*)

OAS 4 *The Who (And Others).* 15 October 1967. (Not in *GOD* or *3DI*)

THE OSIRIS 400 SERIES

OA 401 *Hapshash And The Coloured Coat.* Hapshash And The Coloured Coat. Double size silkscreen. 1967. This is a poster for the first album (Minit 40001) by English, Waymouth, record producer Guy Stevens and heavy friends. Hapshash also designed the album sleeve. The sleeve features original full-colour designs, both front and back, plus a black and silver insert photograph of the trio, all designed by Hapshash. (*3DI* 25, *GOD* 36)

There was only one item in the 400 series.

THE OSIRIS 500 SERIES

OA 501 *Arthur Brown.* Designer unknown. Offset. 1967(?). Black and white photograph with coloured psychedelic eyes. (*GOD* 46)

OA 502 *Jimi Hendrix.* Designer unknown. Offset. 1967(?). Black and white photograph. (Not in *GOD* or *3DI*)

OA 503 *Che Guevara.* Designer unknown. Offset. 1967(?). Black and white photograph, reduced to line shot on PMT machine. (Not in *GOD* or *3DI*)

There were only three items in the 500 series.

THE OSIRIS 600 SERIES

OA 601 *Unknown.*

OA 602 *Buy Granny Takes A Trip And Join The Brain-Drain.* Hapshash And The Coloured Coat. Silkscreen. 1968. Despite the title, this poster is not a promo for the Purple Gang record; rather it is for Waymouth's boutique, Granny Takes A Trip. (*3DI* 31)

It is not known whether there are any other posters in the 600 series.

RELATED POSTERS

The following posters are thought to be connected with Osiris.

14-Hour Technicolor Dream. Hapshash And The Coloured Coat. Silkscreen. 1967. This poster exists in at least three formats. A huge (five feet high) billboard version, in black and white plus a full-colour one that exists normal size and in a reduced handbill size.

14-Hour Technicolor Dream. Mike McInnerney. Silkscreen. 1967.

Fairport Convention? If I Had A Ribbon Bow. Artists unknown. Offset(?). 1967. A promo poster for Track Records. Tim Buckley and others at Middle Earth.

Hapshash And The Coloured Coat. Silkscreen. 1968. (*GOD* 50, *3DI* 25)

First International Pop Festival, Rome. Hapshash And The Coloured Coat. 1968. (*GOD* 53, *3DI* 30)

Arthur Brown Game. Mike McInnerney. Silkscreen. 1967. I have no recollection of this poster, consequently I don't know if it is literally some sort of poster game or whether it is a gig poster featuring AB and the relatively unknown UK band, The Game.

Arthur Brown/Devil's Grip. Photographer unknown. Offset. 1968(?). Promo poster for Track Records.

Breezes. Designer: OMP. Silkscreen. 1968(?). Poster for a clothes boutique in Brighton.

Michael McClure/The Beard. Michael English. Offset. 1968. Full colour poster for the production of the play at The Royal Court Theatre, London.

Summer Sadness For John Hopkins. Michael English. Offset. 1967. Published as a single sheet special issue of *IT*, when John Hopkins, one of the paper's founders, was jailed on dope charges.

IT, Easter 1967. Mike McInnerney. Offset. Another *IT* single sheet special issue.

Incredible String Band At The Royal Festival Hall. Nigel Waymouth. Offset. November 1969. This poster has no direct association with Osiris. It is included because it is the only known rock or rock-related poster by Nigel Waymouth after he split from Michael English. Less elaborate than the Hapshash work, it is nonetheless recognisably in their style and may be the last example of English psychedelic poster art. The central image is a nineteenth century photograph of a woman (possibly a modern photo, treated to appear nineteenth century) with her lips and nails coloured red. The border is a red, orange and black checker design. The white rectangle at the bottom contains the venue and the date. My copy is for the Festival Hall, London, but I have seen another copy for the Dome in Brighton, suggesting that it was a generic tour poster with versions existing for other venues.

🎧 The authors
with Stanley Mouse,
San Francisco – 1998